THE YANKEES FANATIC

THE YANKEES FANATIC

EDITED BY RANDY HOWE

THE LYONS PRESS
Guilford, Connecticut
An imprint of The Globe Pequot Press

The Lyons Press is an imprint of The Globe Pequot Press.

10 9 8 7 6 5 4 3 2 1

Printed in the United States of America

Designed by Linda R. Loiewski

ISBN 978-1-59921-100-8

Library of Congress Cataloging-in-Publication Data is available on file.

Baseball is a family game and so this book is for my family:
Sally, David, and Chuck Howe, Yankees fanatics all.

CONTENTS

The author wishes to acknowledge the efforts of Jenn Taber, Josh Rosenberg, Alicia Solis, and everyone at The Lyons Press.

FANATIC STATS

According to a 2006 Quinnipiac University poll of more than one thousand registered New York City voters, 48 percent of New Yorkers are Yankees fans and 36 percent are Mets fans. Forty-three percent of men like the Mets, while 41 percent like the Yanks, but women favor the Bronx Bombers 52 percent to 30 percent. Good work, ladies!

LEADING OFF: YANKEES PRIDE

When I got married, I gave each groomsman a personalized gift. For my brother, it was a Yankees jersey. Pinstripes and interlocking NY, just as you'd expect, except I didn't put a number on the back. I left it up to him but will admit to being pleased when he told me he was going with number 15.

All Yankees fans worth their salt know that that's Thurman Munson's number. We all remember how much he meant to the team and how his death so deeply affected every player and fan. The passing of time has done little to diminish the emotions; twenty years later, there was my brother choosing number 15 for his Yankees jersey. That's what I call respect. That's what I call Yankees pride.

It's also pretty respectable that there are so many jersey numbers to pick from. If we were Royals fans my brother would have had a choice between George Brett and . . . George Brett. Who wants to wear a Hal McRae jersey?

Amos Otis? Al Hrabosky? Dan Quisenberry? No other team can boast as many potential jersey numbers because no other team has had as many batting champs, Most Valuable Players, and Hall of Famers. No other team can claim as many pennants or World Series championships.

And in saying "no other team," that includes all teams in all professional sports. As a franchise, the Yankees have experienced far more success than any other ball club. Although there have been bumps in the road, that's all they were. Bumps. Sure, it was disappointing to fall to the Tigers in 2006, but not to be lost in that loss is the fact that the Yankees earned a place in the postseason for the eleventh year in a row. New York is just too driven to settle for less. The owners, save one (CBS), have always refused to accept anything less than a ring ceremony and so have the team's general managers and managers. If somebody in a leadership position didn't fit the bill, that person was cut loose—replaced with someone who had the potential to satisfy the New York fans and media. And the same has been true with the players. Put up the numbers or take your JV skills elsewhere. Fans have too much Yankees pride to put up with mediocrity. The reasons we all love this team are its unrelenting focus on quality; its refusal to be satisfied with a division title; its insistence on developing players in the minors while pursuing the best free agents on the market; and its ability to parlay revenue from concessions, luxury boxes, and the YES Network into the best team money can buy. My brother didn't go to some inexpensive seamstress to get that 15 stitched onto his jersey and you won't ever find Yankees management in a dollar store.

And no, I'm not embarrassed to say "best team money can buy." I'm no apologist. As long as Yankees management is playing within the rules, what's the problem? Instead of questioning our practices and policies, ask what your team's management is doing with the revenue check we sent them. I know what the Tigers, Twins, and A's do with it. They're among the little number of small-market teams that have figured it out. They work to be competitive. So do the Yankees.

In this book, we'll look back at just how competitive the Yankees have been, at just how good they were, and how good they are now. First, are those Yankees of the past, including, of course, the Babe and the pride of the Yankees, Lou Gehrig, plus all the other old-timers. Next is a celebration of the Yankees who have treated us to this current run of excellence. The year of 1996 is where I draw the distinction between yesteryear and today. Eleven years before this book's publication, Joe Torre brought the World Series trophy home to the Bronx for the first time in a long while and it's been a lot of fun for us Yankees fanatics ever since. In 1996, my all-time favorite ballplayer, Don Mattingly, retired, but there was plenty to feel happy about as postseason baseball once again become a regular occurrence in The Bronx. Not a bad trade-off.

After focusing on the players, I pay tribute to the team's leadership, from the management to The Boss himself. There have been other Yankees owners, but you won't find much about them here. Not only is George Steinbrenner larger than life, his ring collection is more than one hand can handle. In my lifetime, he's delivered six championships and for this I am thankful. I also give him an inordinate amount of props because he paid less, out of pocket, for the Yankees than I did for my house and he now sits atop one of the most valued franchises in all of sports, an accomplishment on par with those twenty-six championship teams! The Boss is also staking claim to be larger than The Stadium itself and our next chapter pays tribute to a historic monument whose days are unfortunately numbered. What book with the title *The Yankees Fanatic* would be complete without a few pages dedicated to The House That Ruth Built?

Since our team plays in New York, I had to include some quotes from famous people. From the media, too. Some of the most memorable calls in Yankees history can be found here, including several different takes on Bucky Dent's big blast in Beantown. Mel Allen gets his due, as well. In the spirit of fairness, opponents and Yankees haters get a chapter all their own. Some actually pay reverence, but most just say things we can laugh at. Yankees fans should be above laughing at others, but the way Yankees haters trash us and our team, I say they asked for it. So, I don't want to hear any whining when we give it to them. Right, Pedro?

Sprinkled throughout the book, you'll find Yankees Stats and Yankees Trivia, sure to be a learning experience for even the wisest of diehards out there. And for those whose competitive juices get flowing for trivia, you'll be pleased to know I've included some questions to test your Yankees knowledge. If you fail, it doesn't mean you're any less of a fan—just that you need to brush up on your history a little. Your Yankees history.

As the book begins to wind down, there is information for those who want to do things like put a message up on the scoreboard and maybe even sing the National Anthem before first pitch. For those of you who love your Yankees but can't make it to The Stadium, there's also fan club information. Essentially, anything the Yankees fan wants, he or she will find it in this book. This book. This book, it smells like the sweat inside Jason Giambi's cap. This book, its pages will leave rosin on your fingertips. Each time you turn to a new chapter, there's the sound of thousands of cheering fans raining down from the upper decks, of Eddie Layton jamming on the Hammond organ, of Robert Merrill and Ronan Tynan filling The Stadium with song, of Bob Sheppard's public address announcements echoing off the Bronx County Courthouse with the solidity of granite and the perfection of glass. With each new quote, you can practically taste the cold Budweiser; with each bit of trivia, the Yankees franks. *The Yankees Fanatic* might not be as much fun as a trip to The House That Ruth Built, but it will surely satisfy the Yankees fan, the Yankees fanatic, in all of us.

THE YANKEES FANATIC

THE YANKEES FANATIC

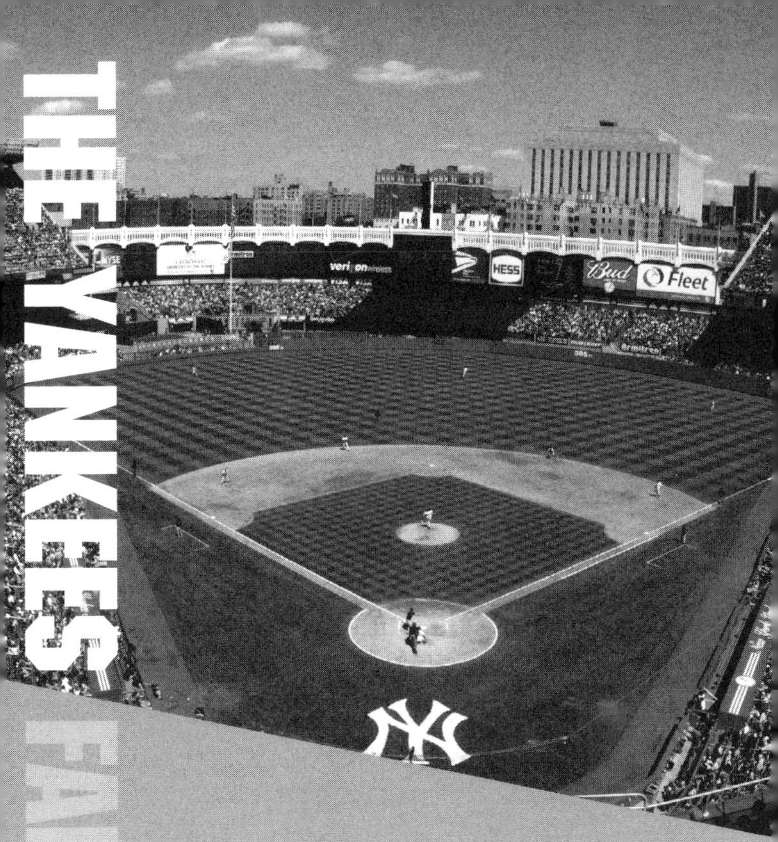

YANKEES OF THE PAST

I want to be a regular player. I'll win more games playing in the outfield than I will pitching every fourth day. And everybody knows that.

BABE RUTH, ARGUING WITH RED SOX OWNER HARRY FRAZEE

Someday, Tiger Woods will be more myth than reality for young golf aficionados. Michael Jordan will be known because of highlight reels, restaurants, and his short shorts. Tom Brady will be recognized as the announcer with the perfect hair and bright white teeth and not as a dynasty quarterback. Wayne Gretzky will forever be referred to as "The Great One," but very few will know just how many of his points came on assists. Behind every legend, there's something real. There are the details of the work they put in even as their accomplishments were being chiseled into trophies and etched into plaques. The same is true of all those Yankees greats.

Pride grows out of hard work and achievement and when considering Yankees of the past, there is reason for great pride. That's why you won't find any goofy Yogi Berra quotes in this book. Not only has that horse been beaten to death too, too many times, I have no interest in belittling the man. Yogi Berra's no joke. He won three MVP awards. As a catcher. He was named to the American League all-star team fifteen times, had more home runs than strikeouts in five different seasons, and was instrumental in ten World Series championships. Ten!!! That's more rings than Jordan and Brady have. Combined! So, if you're hoping for another rehash of Yogi's malapropisms, look somewhere else. When I think about the Yankees forefathers, I think about them with reverence and awe. If I want to laugh, I'll watch a Devil Rays highlight film.

I could've written a whole book about Berra and the same could be said of most Yankees Hall of Famers. And why would these books be interesting? Because each of these Yankees started out as a nobody before becoming a "somebody." Each of these Yankees showed up at the ballpark on game day, laced up the spikes, and faced off against an able opponent. And more times than not, they beat that opponent. Each of these Yankees was a player before becoming a legend.

Lou Gehrig lived and breathed and then one day—one day way too soon—he was gone, but not before making the most famous speech in all of sports. And yes, I think it was the most famous speech because it transcended sports. It was the Iron Horse displaying all the iron he had left before leaving the field of play. That other famous Yankee of the 1920s and '30s might have lacked the Ivy League education of Gehrig, but made up for it by being larger than life. And by hitting more home runs than anyone before him. It was Babe Ruth who put the franchise on the map. The "Bronx Bomber" nickname didn't come from Phil "Scooter" Rizzuto's sacrifice bunts, nor did it come from Derek Jeter's sacrifice flies. No, it was guys like Ruth and Mickey Mantle and the original straw to stir the drink, Mr. October himself, Reggie Jackson. Even when Reggie missed the pitch, corkscrewing himself into the ground after a vicious cut, it sent a message: I'm gonna make you pay. That's the Bronx Bomber way.

Just ask the Dodgers if they ever laughed at one of Yogi's quotes or at one of Reggie's swings. Betcha they say no.

Some Yankees greats went to war with a bat in their hands, others did it with their arm. Whitey Ford had to hit the target just like anyone else who's ever toed the rubber. And just like every other pitcher, he was still expected to do it after throwing a hundred pitches. In 1978, I watched Louisiana Lightnin' dig deep like that. He hit the mitt time and again while making those Angel bats miss, miss, miss. Guidry earned his way into a starting role, getting called up as a reliever, and then he earned himself a Cy Young by winning twenty-five games. That night in June, when we all rose as one—more than eighteen times we rose to our feet—to applaud each two-strike count, that was real. As real as the arm fatigue that gnawed at Guidry during the one-game playoff against Boston, as real as the shoulder problems that ended his career. While my father drove the family home that night, Guidry was icing in the clubhouse. Just like any other pitcher. Except in his case, he was a Yankees pitcher. And Yankees pitchers have to have a little left in the tank for October. Guidry was tired, but he pitched well enough to end Boston's season and send the team to the postseason. Another pennant for the Yankees flagpole. Another brick in the Yankees foundation.

Each pennant, each player, is a brick in that foundation, a foundation built on the kind of excellence that leads to rings on the finger and plaques in Cooperstown. The Yankees of the past are the foundation of baseball because the history of the Yankees *is* the history of baseball.

Yankees Trivia

The nickname "Murderer's Row" is associated with the 1927 Yankees but was first used in reference to the team during the 1918 season.

I copied Jackson's style because I thought he was the greatest hitter I had ever seen, the greatest natural hitter I ever saw. He's the guy who made me a hitter.

BABE RUTH, PAYING TRIBUTE TO "SHOELESS" JOE JACKSON

Never let the fear of striking out keep you from swinging.

BABE RUTH

I swing big, with everything I've got. I hit big or I miss big.

BABE RUTH

Yankees Trivia

Yogi Berra is one of just six managers to lead teams in both the National League and the American League to the World Series.

So far as this year is concerned, there is just one thing that makes me think I can better the 59 mark, and that's Lou Gehrig. Having him follow me in the batting order has helped me a lot this year.

BABE RUTH

Yankees Trivia

Bobby Veach is the only man to ever pinch-hit for Babe Ruth. He did so on August 9, 1925.

Ruth was being ridden by the Cubs the entire series and he would ride them right back. At the time, I did think Babe was pointing to the bleachers, but [shortstop] Frank Crosetti told me no, he put up one finger to indicate he had another strike coming. Babe never denied that he was pointing to the stands. Still it was quite extraordinary to see him point, then hit the very next pitch out of the ballpark.

CHARLIE DEVENS, REMEMBERING THE 1932 WORLD SERIES AND BABE RUTH'S "CALLED SHOT"

Babe Ruth shambled slowly around the bases, shaking his fat shoulders and making remarks of mockery to each infielder as he passed. In the uproar, no one was paying much attention to what happened next. Lou Gehrig came to bat and hit the first pitch to the right field flag post. This was a homerun also. The game was as good as over.

TIME MAGAZINE, OCT. 10, 1932, SUMMARIZING GAME FIVE OF THE 1932 WORLD SERIES

Yankees Trivia

Babe Ruth never won the American League MVP Award, but that's only because the league didn't give the award before 1936. Lou Gehrig was the first player to win it.

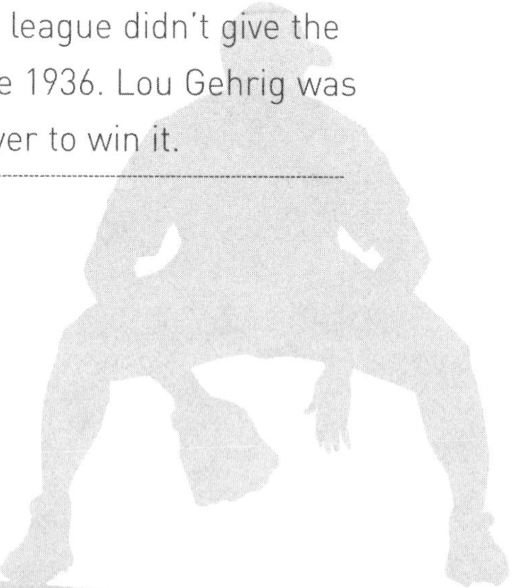

Some 20 years ago, I stopped talking about the Babe for the simple reason that I realized that those who had never seen him didn't believe me.

TOMMY HOLMES

Just one. Whenever I hit a home run, I make certain I touch all four bases.

BABE RUTH, WHEN ASKED IF HE HAD ANY SUPERSTITIONS

Game called by darkness—let the curtain fall. No more remembered thunder sweeps the field. No more the ancient echoes hear the call to one who wore so well sword and shield. The "Big Guy's" left us with the night to face, and there is no one who can take his place.

GRANTLAND RICE, WRITING ABOUT BABE RUTH AND HIS RETIREMENT

The secret of success in pitching lies in getting a job with the Yankees.

WAITE HOYT

It's great to be young and a Yankee.

WAITE HOYT

Huggins was almost like a schoolmaster in the dugout. There was no goofing off. You watched the game, and you kept track not only of the score and the number of outs, but of the count on the batter. At any moment, Hug might ask you what the situation was.

WAITE HOYT

If you had nine Combses on your ball club, you could go to bed every night and sleep like a baby

MILLER HUGGINS, PAYING HOMAGE TO EARLE COMBS

Yankees Trivia

Lou Gehrig broke into the Yankees lineup for good when Wally Pipp had to take a day off after being hit in the head with a pinch during the previous day's batting practice.

The Babe is one fellow, and I'm another and I could never be exactly like him. I don't try, I just go on as I am in my own right.

LOU GEHRIG

Yankees Trivia

"Today, I consider myself the luckiest man on the face of the earth." This line from Lou Gherig in the movie *Pride of the Yankees* was voted number thirty-eight of the all-time greatest movie quotes in a poll conducted by the American Film Institute.

Babe Ruth coached him in batting: in a year or two Gehrig was, next to Ruth, the hardest hitter in the most potent batting machine baseball had ever known.

***TIME* MAGAZINE, OCT. 10, 1932, SUMMARIZING THE 1932 WORLD SERIES**

I worked real hard to learn to play first. In the beginning, I used to make one terrible play a game. Then, I got so I'd make one a week, and finally, I'd pull a real bad one maybe once a month. At the end, I was trying to keep it down to one a season.

LOU GEHRIG

The ballplayer who loses his head, who can't keep his cool, is worse than no ballplayer at all.

LOU GEHRIG

There is no room in baseball for discrimination. It is our national pastime and a game for all.

LOU GEHRIG

It's always the same, **Combs walks, Koenig singles, Ruth hits one out of the park, Gehrig doubles, Lazzeri triples. Then Dugan goes in the dirt on his can.**

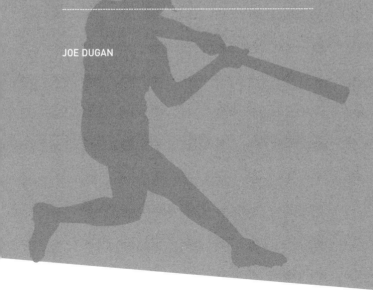

JOE DUGAN

Yankees Trivia

Lou Gehrig delivered his famous "luckiest man alive" speech on July 4, 1939.

Bill Dickey was the heart of the team defensively and commanded tremendous respect from the Yankee pitchers. Once the game started, he ran the show.

BILL WERBER

A catcher must want to catch. He must make up his mind that it isn't the terrible job it is painted, and that he isn't going to say every day, "Why, oh why, with so many other positions in baseball, did I take up this one?"

BILL DICKEY

Bobby Doerr is one of the very few who played the game hard and retired with no enemies.

TOMMY HENRICH

That Ruffing is a wonder. Always in there winning that important game for you.

JIMMIE FOXX, DESCRIBING RED RUFFING

The secret of my success was clean living and a fast moving outfield.

LEFTY GOMEZ

I'm throwing twice as hard but the ball is getting there half as fast.

LEFTY GOMEZ

I talked to the ball a lot of times in my career. I yelled, "Go foul. Go foul."

LEFTY GOMEZ

I was never nervous when I had the ball, but when I let go I was scared to death.

LEFTY GOMEZ

Yankees Trivia

Joe DiMaggio actually played shortstop when he was in high school. Unfortunately, his strong arm led to too many errors.

"He tied the mark at forty-four

July the 1st, you know

Since then he's hit a good twelve more

Joltin' Joe DiMaggio!"

BY BEN HOMER AND ALAN COURTNEY, PERFORMED BY LES BROWN

The phrase, "off with the crack of the bat," while romantic, is really meaningless, since the outfielder should be in motion long before he hears the sound of the ball meeting the bat.

JOE DIMAGGIO

A ball player's got to be kept hungry to become a big-leaguer. That's why no boy from a rich family ever made the big leagues

JOE DIMAGGIO

Yankees Trivia

Joe DiMaggio's fifty-six-game-hit streak began on May 15, 1941, and ended on July 17 of that same year.

You always get a special kick on Opening Day, no matter how many you go through. You look forward to it like a birthday party when you're a kid. You think something wonderful is going to happen.

JOE DIMAGGIO

There is always some kid who may be seeing me for the first or last time, I owe him my best.

JOE DIMAGGIO

One day after striking out, he came into the dugout and kicked the ball bag. We all went "ooooh." It really hurt. He sat down and the sweat popped out on his forehead and he clenched his fists without ever saying a word. Everybody wanted to howl, but he was a god. You don't laugh at gods.

JERRY COLEMAN, RELATING A STORY ABOUT JOE DIMAGGIO

He looks like he's throwing wads of tissue paper. Every time he wins a game, fans come out of the stands asking for contracts.

CASEY STENGEL, DESCRIBING EDDIE LOPAT

Yankees Stats

During Casey Stengel's twelve-year tenure as manager, the Yankees appeared in the World Series ten times and won seven of them.

On the ball field he is perpetual motion itself. He would run through a brick wall, if necessary, to make a catch, or slide into a pit of ground glass to score a run.

ARTHUR DALEY, TALKING ABOUT ENOS SLAUGHTER

In our day with the Yankees, you never used the words, "Nice hustle." That was an insult. . . . We played hard, and that's the reason we won.

GENE WOODLING, REMEMBERING THE YANKEES TEAMS THAT WON FIVE CHAMPIONSHIPS IN A ROW

Yankees Trivia

The year 1951 was pretty amazing for the Yankees. (1) Joe DiMaggio retired. (2) Mickey Mantle made his Yankees debut. (3) Allie Reynolds threw not one but two no-hitters. And (4) the Yankees won their third consecutive world championship.

Heroes are people who are all good with no bad in them. That's the way I always saw Joe DiMaggio. He was beyond question one of the greatest players of the century.

MICKEY MANTLE

In 1960 when Pittsburgh beat us in the World Series, we outscored them 55–27. It was the only time I think the better team lost. I was so disappointed I cried on the plane ride home.

MICKEY MANTLE

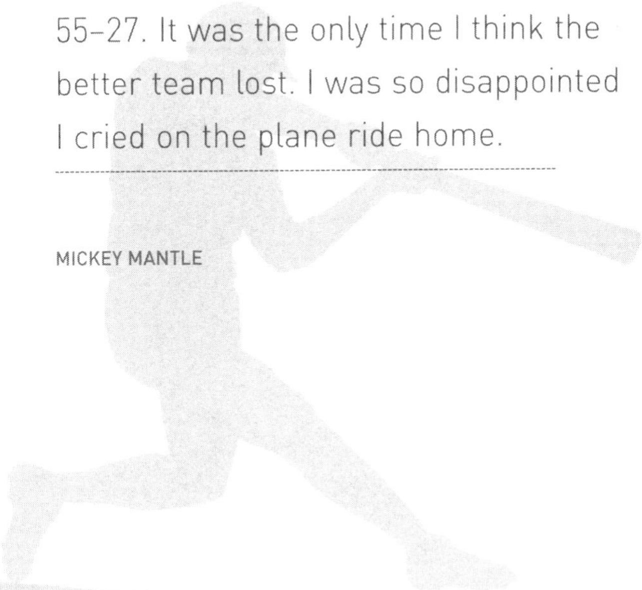

After a home run, I had a habit of running the bases with my head down. I figured the pitcher already felt bad enough without me showing him up rounding the bases.

MICKEY MANTLE

Mantle's greatness was built on power and pain. He exuded the first and endured the second.

ROY FITZGERALD

There is no sound in baseball akin to the sound of Mantle hitting a home run, the crunchy sound of an axe biting into a tree, yet magnified a hundred times in the vast, cavernous, echo making hollows of a ball field.

ARNOLD HANO, *IN BASEBALL STARS* OF 1958

Ladies and gentlemen, a magnificent Yankee, the great number seven, Mickey Mantle.

MEL ALLEN, INTRODUCING MICKEY MANTLE AT MICKEY MANTLE DAY (JUNE 8, 1969)

When he took BP everybody would kind of stop what they were doing and watch.

JIM KAAT, DESCRIBING MICKEY MANTLE

Yankees Stats

Mickey Mantle played eighteen seasons, amassing 536 career home runs.

I never knew how someone dying could say he was the luckiest man in the world. But now I understand.

MICKEY MANTLE

You know, Mantle had the greatest ability of any guy who ever came to the big leagues in my time. He didn't realize how good he was. . . . Mantle could have set unbelievable records. He only used about three-quarters of his talent.

GENE WOODLING

Yankees Stats

During the 1950s, Yankees players were named American League MVP six different times.

I'll take anyway to get into the Hall of Fame. If they want a batboy, I'll go in as a batboy.

PHIL RIZZUTO

My best pitch is anything the batter grounds, lines, or pops in the direction of Rizzuto.

VIC RASCHI

I don't care what the situation was, how high the stakes were—the bases could be loaded and the pennant riding on every pitch, it never bothered Whitey. He pitched his game. Cool. Craft. Nerves of steel.

MICKEY MANTLE, DESCRIBING WHITEY FORD

Yankees Stats

As of 2006, Whitey Ford is the Yankees all-time leader in wins (236), innings pitched (3,171), shutouts (45), and strikeouts (1,956).

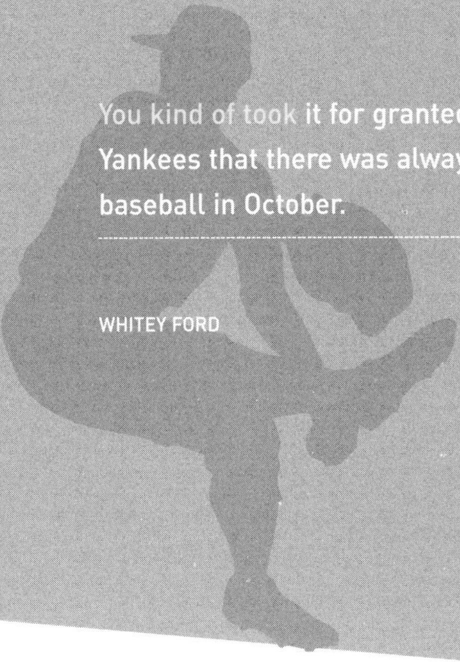

You kind of took it for granted around the Yankees that there was always going to be baseball in October.

WHITEY FORD

So much dignity, so much class.

WHITEY FORD DESCRIBING ELSTON HOWARD,
THE FIRST-EVER BLACK PLAYER FOR THE YANKEES

Elston comes to the Yankees as one of the most heralded rookies in many years. Although he has been a catcher, and is carried on the roster as a catcher, it is thought that he may be converted into an outfielder. It seems he is just too good not to play regularly major league ball, and yet it is hard to displace a veteran as good as Yogi Berra.

FROM ELSTON HOWARD'S 1955 BOWMAN BASEBALL CARD

Why has our pitching been so great? Our catcher that's why. He looks cumbersome but he's quick as a cat.

CASEY STENGEL, DISCUSSING YOGI BERRA

The toughest man in the league in the last three innings.

PAUL RICHARDS, DESCRIBING YOGI BERRA'S LATE-INNING HEROICS

Yankees Trivia

A philosophy professor named Paul Laurendeau has actually written about Yogi's malapropisms. His article is titled, "An Inquiry into a Sample of Vernacular Philosophy: The Aphorisms of Yogi Berra," and can be found at www.yorku.ca/paull/textes/yogiberra.html.

Talking to Yogi Berra about baseball is like talking to Homer about the Gods.

A. BARTLETT GIAMATTI

The game is supposed to be fun. If you have a bad day, don't worry about it. You can't expect to get a hit every game.

YOGI BERRA

Nothing came easy to me. I had to think things over and over more than guys with natural ability did.

JOHNNY SAIN

Everyone asks how I felt before the perfect game. You never feel bad when you're in the World Series. You've got all winter to rest.

DON LARSEN, ON HIS PERFECT GAME IN THE 1956 WORLD SERIES

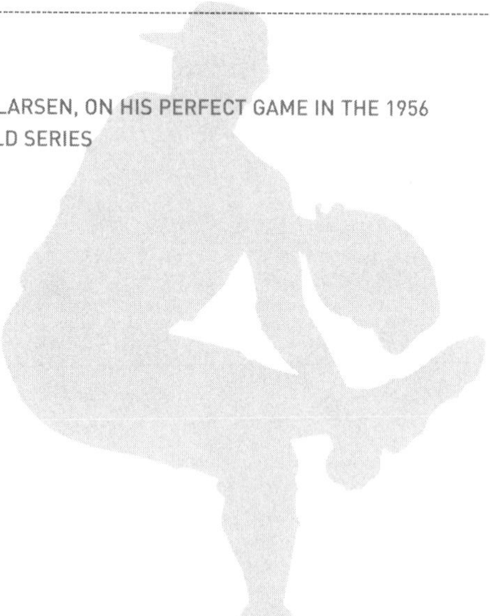

Put up or shut up your damn ass. Let's settle this under the stands right now!

BILLY MARTIN, MAKING AN ELOQUENT OFFER TO JIMMY PIERSALL OF THE RED SOX

I may not have been the greatest Yankee to put on the uniform, but I was the proudest.

BILLY MARTIN

Guys on the street shook hands and said they'd miss me, and the first time I came to bat for Kansas City in Yankee Stadium, they gave me a terrific hand. I just want to tell them all, "Thanks."

BILLY MARTIN, RETURNING TO NEW YORK FOR THE FIRST TIME AFTER BEING TRADED TO THE KANSAS CITY A'S

It was a pleasure to watch the infield play. You couldn't get a ground ball through them. Seeing them was like looking at a work of art.

JIM OGLE, DESCRIBING THE YANKEES INFIELD OF 1961

This was the most selfless team I ever managed. We thought about only one thing, winning the pennant. No one worried much about their batting average or how many runs they were driving in.

RALPH HOUK, PROUDLY TALKING ABOUT HIS 1961 YANKEES

Yankees Stats*

In 1991, Commissioner Faye Vincent made Roger Maris's home run record official, removing forever the asterisk from the number 61.

Roger Maris was as good a man and as good a ballplayer as there ever was.

MICKEY MANTLE

I'm not trying to replace him. The record is there and damn right I want to break it, but that isn't replacing Babe Ruth.

ROGER MARIS

When Roger Maris was going for the home run record he would eat only bologna and eggs for breakfast. Every morning we would have breakfast together at the Stage Deli in Manhattan. We had the same waitress, and I'd leave her the same five-dollar tip every time. After, I would drive Roger up to the Stadium.

JULIE ISAACSON

When he hit the 61st home run I screamed so loud I had a headache for about a week.

PHIL RIZZUTO

If I never hit another home run—this is the one they can never take away from me.

ROGER MARIS, DESCRIBING NUMBER 61

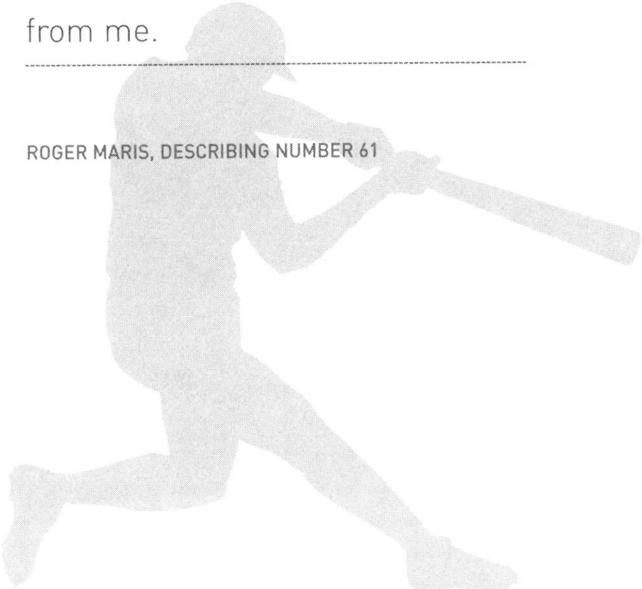

When you're a 25-year-old kid and your dream has always been to play professional baseball, it's kind of hard to believe. When you look around and you see all of these great players, it's hard to fathom that you're in the middle of all that and that you're taking a role in that situation. Out of everybody in the country, how come I was the one playing in Yankee Stadium, standing there with my locker next to Mickey Mantle's, going out to dinner with Bobby Richardson after a game? It was just a great feeling.

TOM TRESH

Yankees Trivia

In 1962, Tom Tresh won the American League Rookie of the Year award.

Clete Boyer to my mind was the finest third baseman that ever lived. Better than Brooks Robinson, better than Graig Nettles, I don't think I ever saw a third baseman who had as much range as Clete Boyer.

RICHARD LALLY

[Bobby] Murcer was a very underrated player. He was a terrific player. . . . Bill James doing his historical abstracts is causing Murcer to get that much more credit for being the player that he was.

RICHARD LALLY

Competing in sports has taught me that if I'm not willing to give 120 percent, somebody else will.

RON BLOMBERG

Come on back to the bench, you aren't supposed to stay out here.

ELSTON HOWARD TO RON BLOMBERG AFTER THE INNING IN WHICH BLOMBERG BECAME THE FIRST DESIGNATED HITTER IN BASEBALL

A lot of long relievers are ashamed to tell their parents what they do. The only nice thing about it is that you get to wear a uniform like everybody else.

JIM BOUTON

You spend a good piece of your life gripping a baseball, and in the end it turns out that it was the other way around all the time.

JIM BOUTON

If you're not having fun in baseball, you miss the point of everything.

CHRIS CHAMBLISS

On the day I was signed, Mr. Finley, the owner of the Athletics at that time came up to me and said, "When you were six you ran away from home, and when your parents found you at a nearby lake, you had already caught two catfish and were pulling in a third. Now repeat it back to me."

CATFISH HUNTER, DESCRIBING HOW HE GOT HIS NICKNAME

Just two words: **a masterpiece.**

JOE DIMAGGIO, COMMENTING ON CATFISH HUNTER'S PERFECT GAME IN 1968

To be a Yankee is a thought in everyone's head. . . . Just walking into Yankee Stadium, chills run through you. I believe there was a higher offer, but no matter how much money is offered, if you want to be a Yankee, you don't think about it.

CATFISH HUNTER

This 20th win means more to me than the perfect game in 1968.

CATFISH HUNTER

The reason I'm a Yankee is that George Steinbrenner out hustled everybody else.

REGGIE JACKSON, AFTER SIGNING WITH THE YANKEES IN 1976

He'd give you the shirt off his back. Of course he'd call a press conference to announce it.

CATFISH HUNTER, ON REGGIE JACKSON

Out of what . . . a thousand?

MICKEY RIVERS, COMMENTING ON REGGIE JACKSON'S CLAIM OF HAVING AN IQ OF 160

There's a difference **between a good player and a good player in New York.**

REGGIE JACKSON

So many ideas come to you and you want to try them all, but you can't. You're like a mosquito in a nudist colony, you don't know where to start.

REGGIE JACKSON, TRYING TO BREAK OUT OF A SLUMP

This team is loaded with tough guys. This team is loaded with professionals.

REGGIE JACKSON, DESCRIBING THE 1978 YANKEES

When I'm at bat, I'm in scoring position.

OSCAR GAMBLE

Yankees Stats

On July 18, 1978, Ron Guidry struck out eighteen California Angels. At one point he even K'ed twelve of thirteen batters.

There's a hate-respect thing between us. We didn't like each other at all, but we had a respect for the great players Boston had. That's part of what makes the Yankees and Red Sox special. I'd heard about the rivalry when I was with the White Sox, but you don't know about it until you play in it and feel the electricity of the crowd.

BUCKY DENT

I had a dream as a kid. I dreamed some day I would hit a home run to win something.

BUCKY DENT

When I hit the ball, I knew that I had hit it high enough to hit the wall. But there were shadows on the net behind the wall and I didn't see the ball land there. I didn't know I had hit a homer until I saw the umpire at first signaling home run with his hand. I couldn't believe it.

BUCKY DENT, DISCUSSING HIS THREE-RUN HOME RUN IN 1978'S ONE-GAME PLAYOFF AGAINST THE RED SOX

That '78 playoff game is something I'll never forget. . . . It was probably the most exciting game I ever played in.

LOU PINIELLA

I just remember that when Bucky hit the ball there was a deafening hush over the crowd. Thirty thousand people just totally shocked.

WILLIE RANDOLPH

Yankees Trivia

Willie Randolph was involved in two successful hidden ball tricks: once as the trickster and once as the tricked! He got Bump Wills out and then it was pulled on him two seasons later.

And now for the varsity.

GRAIG NETTLES, AS THE RED SOX WERE LEAVING THE FIELD AND THE YANKEES WERE PREPARING TO TAKE IT

Why pitch nine innings when you can get just as famous pitching two?

SPARKY LYLE

A mystique of history and heritage surrounds the New York Yankees. It's like the old days revived. We're loved and hated, but always in larger doses than any other team. We're the only team in any sport whose name and uniform and insignia are synonymous with their entire sport all over the world. . . . The Yankees mean baseball to more people than all the other teams combined.

PAUL BLAIR

I had set the standard for my style of relief pitching so high that when I came back to the rest of the pack, everybody said I was done. I was so aggressive on the mound and thought I could throw the ball by anyone. I was so high up there in terms of how I went about my job and being overpowering.

GOOSE GOSSAGE

Gossage was this easy-going guy until the eighth inning. Then you'd see this metamorphosis occur. All of a sudden he looked like a wild man.

BARRY FOOTE

I remember the first time I caught him he'd gotten behind on the hitter and there was a runner on first, so I step out in front of the plate to say something and he yells, "Get your ass back there and catch." Finally I go back, Goose throws three straight strikes and we're out of the inning.

BARRY FOOTE

Gossage was amazingly good for amazingly long.

ALEX BELTH, *SPORTS ILLUSTRATED*, DEC. 16, 2005

Yankees Trivia

Thurman Munson was the first Yankee to win the Rookie of the Year and MVP awards.

I like hitting fourth and I like the good batting average. But what I do every day behind the plate is a lot more important because it touches so many more people and so many more aspects of the game.

THURMAN MUNSON

Thurman was indispensable and irreplaceable.

GEORGE STEINBRENNER

Thurman was one of the things you could always count on.

BILLY MARTIN

Fisk is in the Hall of Fame, and I think had Thurman not had that unfortunate accident, he'd be there too. They were simply the two very best catchers of that era.

LOU PINIELLA

Growing up, I kind of liked the way he played. I didn't see much of him, but I remember him being a leader. I remember him really standing up for his teammates, and that really caught my eye.

JORGE POSADA, DESCRIBING THURMAN MUNSON

Yankees Trivia

On August 2, 1979, Thurman Munson was killed while flying his plane home to Ohio.

The case for Tommy John is a bit too reliant on the fact that he stuck around for 26 years rather than having an exceptionally high peak, but if you consider the hundreds of pitchers whose careers have been salvaged by the pioneering surgical procedure which bears his name, his case for a bronze plaque becomes much stronger.

JAY JAFFE, ARGUING FOR TOMMY JOHN'S INDUCTION INTO THE HALL OF FAME

The handsome hurler walked four and struck out nine men, including Wade Boggs for the final out. Boggs, hitting .357 at the time, went down swinging on a hard slider.

HARVEY FROMMER, DESCRIBING DAVE RIGHETTI'S NO-HITTER OF JULY 4, 1983

I didn't look in the dugout because I didn't want to get more nervous. But I calmed down. I was enjoying the fans. I was enjoying being a Yankee.

DAVE RIGHETTI, DISCUSSING HIS NO-HITTER

Yankees Stats

The following are the Yankees American League batting champions as of 2006: Babe Ruth (1924 .378); Lou Gehrig (1934 .363); Joe DiMaggio (1939 .381; 1940 .352); Snuffy Stirnweiss (1945 .309); Mickey Mantle (1956 .353); Don Mattingly (1984 .343); Paul O'Neill (1994 .359); Bernie Williams (1998 .339).

Now it's on to May, and you know about me and May.

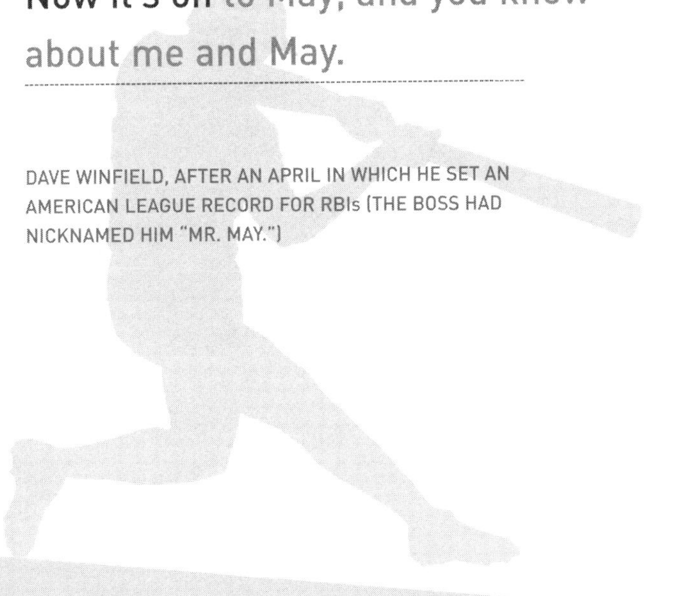

DAVE WINFIELD, AFTER AN APRIL IN WHICH HE SET AN AMERICAN LEAGUE RECORD FOR RBIs (THE BOSS HAD NICKNAMED HIM "MR. MAY.")

I feel very fortunate to have played with him, coached him, and managed him. He was a great player.

LOU PINIELLA, DISCUSSING DON MATTINGLY

What did I do to deserve this?

DON MATTINGLY, ON DON MATTINGLY DAY
(AUGUST 31, 1997)

Honestly, at one time I thought Babe Ruth was a cartoon character. I really did, I mean, I wasn't born until 1961, and I grew up in Indiana.

DON MATTINGLY

I'm glad I don't have to face that guy every day. He has that look that few hitters have. I don't know if it is in his stance, his eyes or what. But you can tell he means business.

DWIGHT GOODEN, TALKING ABOUT DON MATTINGLY

Baseball's still a game. I don't want it to be work. I want it to be a game.

DON MATTINGLY

Yankees Stats

As of 2006, Lou Gehrig is the Yankees all-time leader in doubles. Bernie Williams is second on the list and Don Mattingly is third.

THE YANKEES FANATIC

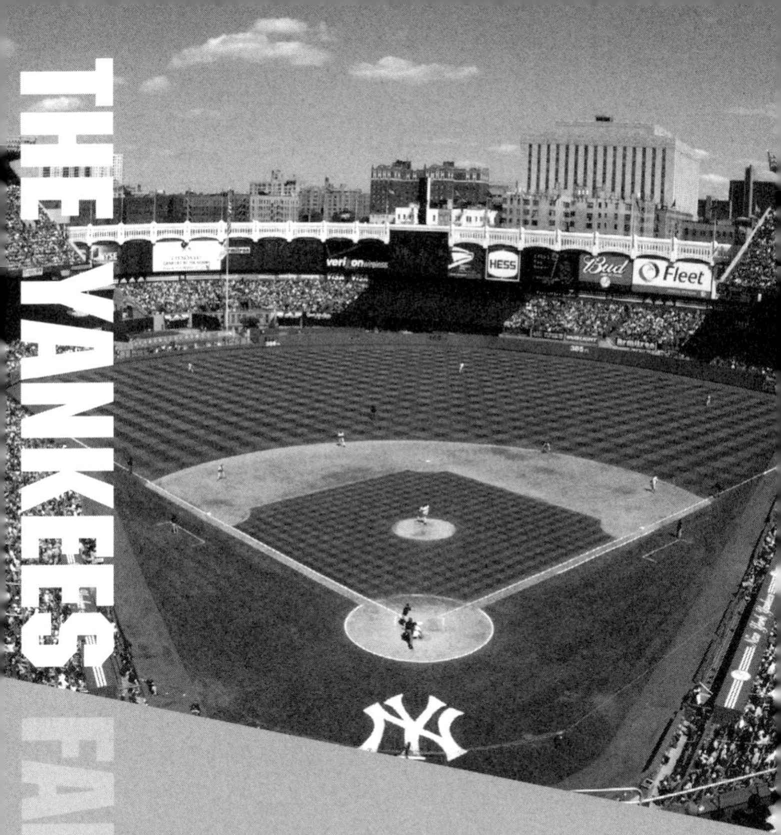

A SPEECH FROM
AMERICA'S MAYOR

On October 29, 1996, New York Mayor Rudolph Giuliani gave a speech at City Hall after the Yankees finished their parade through the Canyon of Heroes. The celebration commemorated the first World Series championship for the Yankees in eighteen years. The following is excerpted from that speech:

The 1996 season began in the snows of April, and ends today in the bright sunlight of a New York October. Once upon a time, October meant World Championships for New York City, and this great 1996 Yankee team has once again made October in New York City a magic time of heroic achievement, a championship season.

The New York Yankees are the greatest franchise in sports, and New York is the greatest city in the world—and the capital of the world. The Yankees have created much of the history and legend of baseball, and now this 1996 Yankee team has written a new and glorious chapter in that history and legend. Like New Yorkers themselves, this team plays best under pressure. Remember just one week ago today, the Yankees trailed the Braves 2–0, and all the experts said the Yanks couldn't do it. Well, as they did against Texas, and against Baltimore. As they did all year, the Yankees came from behind and they won four of the most exciting games ever. And their victory is an inspiration for all of us. It is a metaphor for a city whose people perform best under pressure. It is a metaphor for a city that is undergoing a great renaissance.

Today we celebrate the achievement of an entire team. They won as a team. Today we thank George Steinbrenner for bringing to our city yet another Yankee World Championship. And we thank George Steinbrenner for his commitment, his vision, and his courage in sticking with his ballplayers, even against the advice of many of the critics and experts. Indeed, even as we celebrate the greatest victory in the world of baseball, and a terrific season, it is the human victories that most capture our hearts and our imaginations. The victory of manager Joe Torre . . . Joe Torre from Brooklyn, New York, whose calmness, courage, love and never-say-die attitude set the tone for his entire team. The entire Torre family symbolizes the spirit of New York with their commitment, and their love of each other and of this Yankee ball club. From Joe's brothers, the dearly loved and departed Rocco Torre, and Frank, who has just received a new heart, to Joe's sisters, Marguerite Torre and Rae Torre, this family is a New York family—a Brooklyn family—it represents to all of us the very best of what New York City is all about. And Bob Watson, the general manager, who had to undergo so much second guessing. It was all worth it as the players he acquired helped to make this great victory possible.

And most of all, we honor the players. This is a team where everyone contributed and no one complained. All the players put their private interests aside in the true team spirit and pulled together to capture the biggest prize of all. And as the pressure increased they just kept getting better, growing in confidence, and realizing that they have the talent to always come back.

This is a great day for the Yankees and their fans, and a great time to be a New Yorker. We are the capital of the world, and the champions of the world, and it just doesn't get any better than that. To our heroes in pinstripes we say thank you for giving us a season we'll never forget and another October to remember.

Thank you.

Today I also want to pay special tribute to our New York Yankees fans. You are the very best. There will be many tributes to you today. You deserve them all. Even the opposing team recognized just how awesome you are. The Braves fine third baseman, Chipper Jones said, "The Yanks have got probably the best fans I've ever seen . . . almost willing their team to make things happen."

He's right. You are the best fans in baseball. In all of sports. . . .

And now, I would like to ask Mr. George Steinbrenner to please come forward. George, in honor of the Yankees championship season, I am honored to present you and the entire team with an official proclamation naming Tuesday, October 29, 1996, as "New York Yankees Day" in the City of New York.

THE YANKEES FANATIC

THE MODERN-DAY YANKEES: FROM 1996'S WORLD CHAMPIONSHIP TO TODAY

The owner of the New York Yankees, Mr. George Steinbrenner who I had the greatest respect for, I want to thank him for giving me the opportunity to win that special ring in 1996.

WADE BOGGS

Between 1982 and 1994, the Bronx suffered through desertification. This is a topographical calamity that takes place when all life is sucked out of an area—in this case, an entire borough. Sand replaces flora and fauna and the landscape looks as odd as an October night with no Goodyear blimp to fly over The Stadium. Desertification means sand dunes, camels, and oases with names like Jesse Barfield, Ken Phelps, and Ed Whitson. Perhaps the worst tease of an oasis came in 1994 as the Yanks were well on their way to the postseason when the players decided to strike. But back to my metaphor, between 1982 and 1994 Yankee Stadium was a desert devoid of pennants, rings, and trophies. It was a drought unlike any other in my lifetime. After losing to the Dodgers in the 1981 World Series, the greatest franchise in all of professional sports went thirteen unlucky years without making it back to the playoffs. A whole generation of newborns turned into teenagers without ever experiencing the joy of seeing that postseason bunting hanging from the upper decks, of seeing that blimp shot of the sold-out Stadium. A whole generation feeling sunburned and snake bit.

For a team like the Red Sox, thirteen years is no big deal. The city of Boston spent eighty-six years doing its best Sahara impersonation. And the Cubby faithful, they've been wandering through the desert even longer! A lot of teams would sign up in a heartbeat for a trip to the postseason every thirteen years. As a boy, I didn't yet appreciate the history of the Yankees. I didn't know that thirteen years was totally and completely unacceptable. I couldn't understand why Steinbrenner got so mad and why so many managers got fired. It was in this climate of mediocrity that I was raised to bleed Yankees blue.

So, when 1995 rolled around and Don Mattingly was finally introduced for Game One of the American League Division Series, I felt the goose bumps. And they were legitimate goose bumps. I don't want to hear from some bitter fans of some second-tier team how small a price I'd paid, how they alone know what pain is, how we have an embarrassment of riches and I should be embarrassed to talk about the losing I experienced as a kid. Hey, from age ten to age twenty-five, I never got to see my team in the Fall Classic! And as a twenty-four-year old, when Don Mattingly batted over .400 against Seattle, I was ecstatic. But with the highs come the lows—watching Ken Griffey slide across home plate meant not only the end of the season but the end of the career of my all-time favorite

Yankee. I was truly heartbroken and no envious critic can ever diminish that emotion.

So anyway, 1995 ended and then 1996 began.

And oh did it ever. Mariano Rivera proved to be our bridge out of the desert. With just one arm raised, Mo could part the sea. Pitching the seventh and eighth innings, Rivera quickly made it apparent to all who were paying attention that the Yanks had a force to be reckoned with. Mariano's cutter led us to the promised land, but it seemed like Atlanta would scorch us quick and easy. Joe Torre had other plans, though. Pettitte won that 1–0 gem in Game Five, and in Game Six John Wetteland earned his fourth save of the series, the Yankees' fourth straight victory, to wrap things up. When Charlie Hayes gripped that pop fly tight, I was gripping the arm of the couch twice as tight. This was no oasis, this was the real deal! The Yankees were once again champions! Little did Yankees fans know that this was the start of a dynasty. After thirteen years, all we could talk about was the here and now.

Like the pile of players piling onto one another on the mound, my friends and I piled into a bar to share in the celebration, and when the piano player took a break, I sneaked behind the keys to play the one song I know: the Yankees theme song. "Na, naaa, nana, nana, nananaaaa." Everybody went nuts and even the piano player, one of these old-school jazzy types in a beret, had to cheer. This was the first of many celebrations. This was the coming-out party for Mo and Jeter, Pettitte and Bernie. This was the beginning of the modern era.

We play today, we win today—das it.

MARIANO DUNCAN, PROVIDING THE YANKEES WITH THEIR 1996 RALLY CRY

It does something to the other team, knowing you've got guys who can come in and just take the game right out of their hands.

JIMMY KEY, DESCRIBING THE YANKEES BULL PEN OF MARIANO RIVERA AND JOHN WETTELAND

There's nobody I'd rather see out there in a big game than Jimmy Key.

DAVID CONE

Everyone is chillin' right now, then when it's game time, it's business. No one here gets overgeeked.

CECIL FIELDER

He's a big **old boy.**

CECIL FIELDER, DESCRIBING HIDEKI IRABU

When I look in the mirror, I look at the enemy. There is no one to blame for this but myself. I should have bought myself a mirror a long time ago.

DARRYL STRAWBERRY, COMMENTING ON HIS RETURN TO BASE-BALL AFTER A DRUG SUSPENSION

Being a line drive hitter sucks.

PAUL O'NEILL, AFTER JUST MISSING A HOME RUN IN THE 1997 PLAYOFF LOSS TO THE INDIANS

You play the game to win the game, and not to worry about what's on the back of the baseball card at the end of the year.

PAUL O'NEILL

Yankees Stats

The 1998 Yankees won 125 regular-season and postseason games (a winning percentage of .714) despite not having one player elected to start in the all-star game.

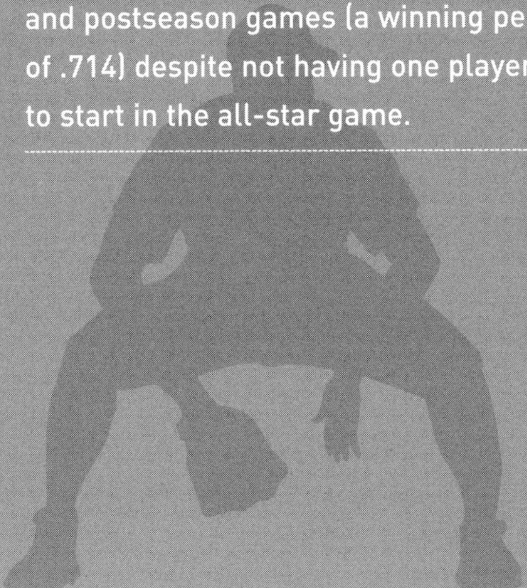

We don't have one big guy. We have a team full of big guys.

TIM RAINES, DESCRIBING THE 1998 YANKEES

There has never been a better team than this one. We created something truly special here.

GEORGE STEINBRENNER, TALKING ABOUT THE 1998 YANKEES AFTER THEY WON THE WORLD SERIES

He's the leader on this team, I know when Baltimore let us have him, they thought they were giving us a problem. I'll take problems like that anytime.

GEORGE STEINBRENNER, DISCUSSING DAVID WELLS AFTER HIS GAME FIVE VICTORY IN THE 1998 AMERICAN LEAGUE CHAMPIONSHIP SERIES

Our staff comes from all over. We have a pitcher from Cuba, a pitcher from Japan, a pitcher from Panama, and Boomer Wells is from Mars.

TINO MARTINEZ

At nighttime, you just try to keep him out of jail.

DAVID CONE, ON DAVID WELLS

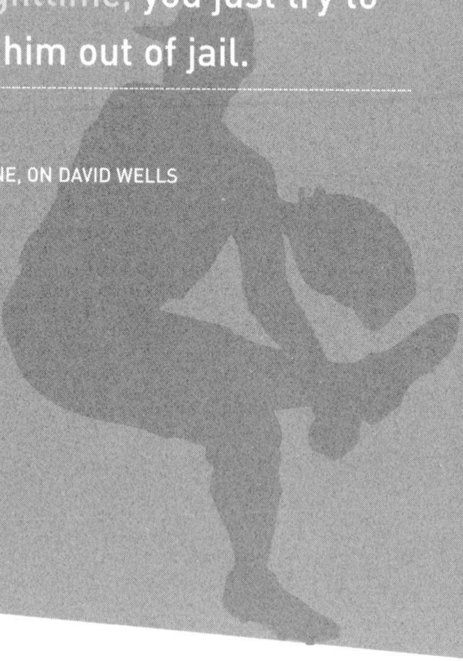

This is kind of special to me. I wish my mom could have seen it. I thought about her after the last out was made.

DAVID WELLS, AFTER PITCHING HIS PERFECT GAME IN 1998

To pitch a perfect game wearing pinstripes at Yankee Stadium, it's unbelievable. Growing up a Yankee fan, to come out here and make history, it really is a dream come true.

DAVID WELLS

I got here late. What happened?

BILLY CRYSTAL, BUSTING BOOMER'S CHOPS IN THE CLUBHOUSE AFTER HIS PERFECT GAME

The shutout doesn't matter. It's the "W." You want to have the "W" instead of the "L."

DAVID WELLS, AFTER GAME ONE OF THE 1998 AMERICAN LEAGUE CHAMPIONSHIP SERIES

I have nothing tonight. Be ready to come in.

DAVID WELLS, TALKING TO CASEY GAYNOR OF THE TOMS RIVER TEAM THAT WON THE LITTLE LEAGUE WORLD SERIES (WELLS CAME WITHIN SEVEN OUTS OF A PERFECT GAME THAT NIGHT)

That was the best two years of my life, in that city, that stadium. That's just kind of hard to take when you're not there anymore.

DAVID WELLS, DISCUSSING HIS TRADE TO THE BLUE JAYS

Everything you hate about New York as a visitor, you love as a home player.

SCOTT BROSIUS

This is the type of thing that as a kid you dream about. Something I've done in my backyard a hundred times. And you never know if you're going to get the opportunity to do it.

SCOTT BROSIUS, DESCRIBING HIS GAME-WINNING HOME RUN IN GAME THREE OF THE 1998 WORLD SERIES

Yankees Stats

Scott Brosius was named the World Series MVP in 1998. He fielded a ground ball for the last out of the Series and was 8 for 17 with 6 RBIs.

Andy is a big game pitcher. That's the bottom line. Every time you think his back is against the wall, he comes out and he does a performance like this. He did it against Texas and he came through again tonight. You can't say enough about him.

DEREK JETER, AFTER GAME FOUR OF THE 1998 WORLD SERIES

It's something inside his heart that's bigger than anything. He's got the heart of a lion about to grab something.

DARRYL STRAWBERRY, TALKING ABOUT DAVID CONE

If you're a student of history, you have to love it. It's 1999 and the Yankees and Red Sox are playing in the postseason for the first time.

DAVID CONE

Yankees Trivia

Andy Pettitte was drafted in the twenty-second round of the 1990 amateur draft.

Never is a concept the Yankees won't ever come across.

ANDY PETTITTE

Hitters get paid a lot of money to hit. Let's face it, man, sometimes they just do.

ANDY PETTITTE

Your pitching coach is almost like your spouse. He's someone to go to when you want to gripe and complain. The big thing for me with Mel is that we've been through so much together. He's been through everything I've been through on the mound. He was a Yankee who won twenty games in New York and a Yankee who didn't win twenty games in New York. For me, he's been there and that's what makes a good pitching coach. He's a good man, too.

ANDY PETTITTE, DISCUSSING MEL STOTTLEMYRE

Yankees Stats

In addition to being a great pitching coach, Mel Stottlemyre was also a highly accomplished pitcher, winning twenty games for the Yanks in 1965, 1968, and 1969.

I never realized how funny he was until I was on the team last year. Matsui is a good guy. He's one of the leaders on the team.

ROBINSON CANO, DISCUSSING HIDEKI MATSUI

I know what kind of pitcher Whitey was, and I know what kind of person Whitey is. It makes me feel proud to be a Yankee. We're keeping this in the family.

MARIANO RIVERA, ON BREAKING WHITEY FORD'S POSTSEASON SCORELESS STREAK

You know in his tone of voice, his facial expressions. When he has a meeting, he doesn't have to scream and yell, he can just give you that face and that tone he has, and you know we had better pick it up and get going again.

TINO MARTINEZ, DESCRIBING JOE TORRE

You probably have a better chance of winning the lottery than this happening, but what an honor.

DAVID CONE, DISCUSSING HIS PERFECT GAME IN 1999

I'm proud to be here. I'm proud to be part of this team . . . but believe me, I lost someone special.

PAUL O'NEILL, AFTER HIS FATHER PASSED AWAY AND HE PLAYED IN GAME FOUR OF THE 1999 WORLD SERIES

Today, when I came to the park, I saw a couple of people that work here. They hugged me. They said, "We love you, but we hate you now."

JOSE VIZCAINO, ON PLAYING AT SHEA AGAINST HIS FORMER TEAM DURING THE 2000 WORLD SERIES

I got a win, in my major-league debut, in Fenway Park, against the Red Sox, in a pennant race. It's the most exciting day of my life.

RANDY KEISLER

The guy's ridiculous. No one hits home runs like that. I'm telling you, man, it's ridiculous.

DEREK JETER, DESCRIBING SHANE SPENCER'S TEN HOME RUNS IN THE REGULAR SEASON AND TWO IN THE POSTSEASON

You gotta have fun. Regardless of how you look at it, we're playing a game. It's a business, it's our job, but I don't think you can do well unless you're having fun.

DEREK JETER

I will never brag about myself, but my family, I can go on forever.

DEREK JETER

Yankees Stats

Between 1996 and 2000, the Yankees won fourteen consecutive World Series games. Between 1998 and 2000, they won nine consecutive postseason series including the American League Division Series, American League Championship Series, and the World Series.

We just want to win—that's the bottom line. I think a lot of times people may become content with one championship or a little bit of success, but we don't really reflect on what we've done in the past. We focus on the present.

DEREK JETER, LOOKING AHEAD TO A SUBWAY SERIES AGAINST THE METS

MVP, you could have picked a name out of a hat. . . . We have a group of MVPs. You don't rely on one guy. You have to get contributions from everyone.

DEREK JETER, ACCEPTING THE 2000 WORLD SERIES MVP AWARD

It's the happiest day of my life. I don't know how to explain it. Today they gave me a chance to come through. I did and it was unbelievable.

LUIS SOJO, AFTER HITTING A TIE-BREAKING SINGLE TO BEAT THE METS IN THE 2000 WORLD SERIES

In case of emergency, break glass and whip him out.

BRIAN CASHMAN, PRAISING LUIS SOJO

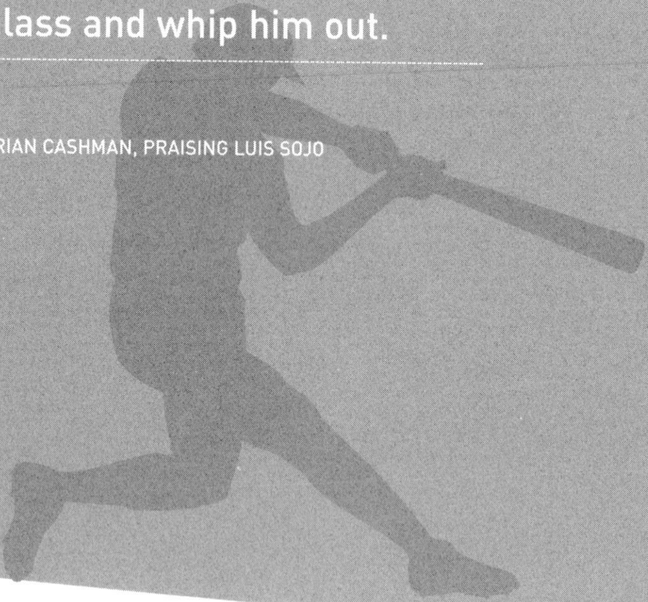

I didn't care how I was hitting as long as we were winning.

BERNIE WILLIAMS, AFTER DEFEATING THE METS IN THE 2000 WORLD SERIES

Yankees Trivia

Bernie Williams chose the number 51 for his jersey to express his opinion that Puerto Rico should become the fifty-first state to join the United States.

Sometimes the hitter get a hit, sometimes I strike them out, but in neither case does anyone die.

ORLANDO HERNANDEZ

I always feel pressure. What I don't have is fear. But pressure, there always is, and whoever says otherwise is lying.

ORLANDO HERNANDEZ, ON PITCHING IN THE POSTSEASON

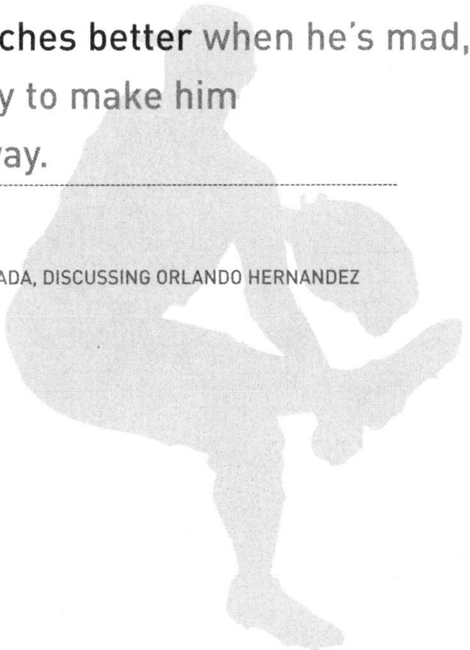

He pitches better when he's mad, so I try to make him that way.

JORGE POSADA, DISCUSSING ORLANDO HERNANDEZ

If it's 90 degrees with 80 percent humidity, Roger is able to say, "So what, I've trained in that. I've trained for that." Actually, his program is harder than the games themselves.

JEFF MANGOLD, YANKEES STRENGTH COACH, DESCRIBING ROGER CLEMENS

Sitting on the bench I saw the ball go over the cutoff man's head and I thought the run was going to score right there. And then Derek came out of nowhere. That was the biggest lift for us.

ANDY PETTITTE, DESCRIBING JETER'S MEMORABLE CUTOFF AGAINST THE A'S

Roger is the one who taught me that the better shape you're in, the better you'll throw the ball. If I've had four good workouts between my starts, I take that confidence to the mound with me. How can it not help me to think that way?

ANDY PETTITTE

He's the one who gave me a chance to get to the World Series. This is where I wanted to be all along. We had a couple of nice offers from other teams, but I tied my agents' hands. I told them I wanted to be a Yankee.

ROGER CLEMENS, DESCRIBING GEORGE STEINBRENNER

Yankees Stats

Roger Clemens and Phil Niekro are the only two pitchers to earn their three-hundredth victory while pitching in pinstripes.

This is a great honor. Captain of the Yankees is not a title that is thrown around lightly. It is a huge responsibility and one that I take very seriously. I thank Mr. Steinbrenner for having such confidence in me.

DEREK JETER, ON JUNE 3, 2003

My dad had been shortstop when he was in college, and you know, when you're a kid, you want to be just like your dad.

DEREK JETER

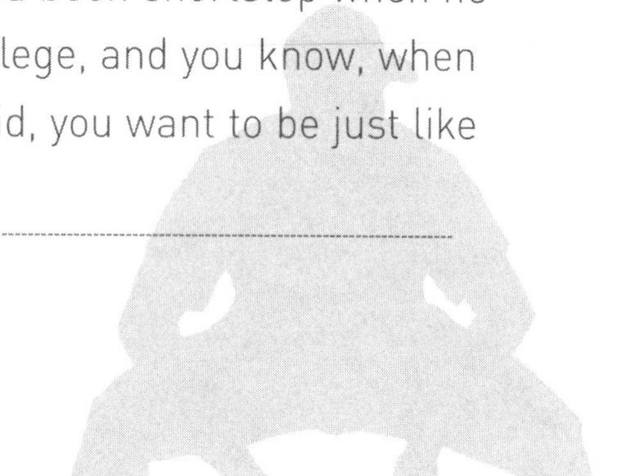

What kind of shortstop is Derek Jeter? Well, a very effective one, to be sure. I think he's a sleeker and leaner model of a Cal Ripken. He's out of the Cal Ripken mold in that he's tall and rangy, has a great arm, covers a lot of ground and he's a great offensive player.

OZZIE SMITH

He'd been summoned by the baseball gods; to carry the torch, to help save the team and the stadium and maybe even the game of baseball itself.

PETER RICHMOND, WAXING POETIC ABOUT DEREK JETER

He gets better every year, that's what's remarkable about him. Some guys are good and stay good. Some guys are good and get better. He reminds me of Kareem. Hubie Brown said that Kareem worked at the beginning of every season to improve some facet of his game. It's that way with the best, whatever the profession. That's the way this kid is.

ED BRADLEY, DESCRIBING DEREK JETER

He's rather unique for a young man in the 1990s. Endowed as he is with all that talent, all that money and such impeccable manners—that makes him an anachronism. In this era of boorish athletes, obnoxious fans, greedy owners and shattered myths, here's a hero who's actually polite, and that has to have come from good parenting.

GAY TALESE, COMMENTING ON DEREK JETER

Ban him from baseball. He should be illegal.

TOM KELLY, DISCUSSING MARIANO RIVERA

Yankees Trivia

In 1998, Bernie Williams won the American League batting title and Joe Torre won Manager of the Year.

I'm not ready to quit my day job.

BERNIE WILLIAMS, AFTER HIS CD, *THE JOURNEY WITHIN*, WAS RELEASED

Where do we go from here? Chico's Bail Bonds on us? Somebody's making money. They're using every place they can to advertise.

MIKE MUSSINA, ON MAJOR LEAGUE BASEBALL'S DECISION TO ALLOW ADVERTISING ON THE BASES

Yankees Trivia

Mike Mussina was born in Williamsport, Pennsylvania, home of the Little League World Series.

The moment he hit it, I knew it was gone.

RUDY GIULIANI, DESCRIBING AARON BOONE'S HOME RUN . . . AGAINST THE RED SOX . . . IN THE THIRTEENTH INNING . . . IN GAME SEVEN . . . OF THE 2003 AMERICAN LEAGUE CHAMPIONSHIP SERIES!

I come out here every day, and my job is important when it comes to being there every day and being there for my pitchers. I really want to be known more as a defensive guy, and take my pitchers to the next level. Every time I go out on the field, I take a lot of pride in what I do at the plate, but I take a lot more pride in what I do behind the plate.

JORGE POSADA

I'm very proud of my area around the plate. I don't want anyone messing with my dirt.

JORGE POSADA

You have to have all types of players to make a clubhouse great. He's the fiery guy. When you think about it, Joe Torre is the calming influence, Derek Jeter leads by example, and Jorge is the fiery guy. When guys need a little kick, Jorge is always there for them.

JOE GIRARDI

He could have been an engineer and he would have been a great one, but he decided to be a catcher and he was a good one. Then he decided to be a bench coach and he was a good one. Now he is going to be a manager and he is going to be a good one.

DON ZIMMER, DISCUSSING JOE GIRARDI AND HIS NEW JOB AS MANAGER OF THE FLORIDA MARLINS

A summer afternoon of baseball ought to be nothing if not relaxing, and no other player can instill calm in his team's fans as reliably as Mariano Rivera, the game's dominant closer and arguably the best relief pitcher of all time.

BUSTER OLNEY

Nobody is immune to being booed. I heard them boo Mickey Mantle. . . . Mariano realizes it's not personal. It's that he didn't do the job. That's the natural thing that comes out in boos. . . . Where much is given, much is expected.

JIM KAAT

I see the hitter when he's moved in the box, like when he's moved closer to the plate or changed his stance. I see when the batter has moved his feet, and then I make my own adjustment.

MARIANO RIVERA

I trust my pitches and I trust my teammates.

MARIANO RIVERA

Without question we're talking about the best reliever, in my opinion, in the history of baseball. This guy has become branded with the Yankee logo. People are going to remember this man for so long for what he's done.

BRIAN CASHMAN, DISCUSSING MARIANO RIVERA

I call Mo "The Equalizer." I mean, I can't tell you how comforting it felt to have him come in when I left the game.

ROGER CLEMENS

He's the most **mentally tough person I've ever played with.**

DEREK JETER, DESCRIBING MARIANO RIVERA

To me, he's the greatest modern day weapon I have seen or played against. He has been the heart and soul of the New York Yankees dynasty.

ALEX RODRIGUEZ, SINGING ALONG TO "ENTER SANDMAN"

Pretty much, you think the game is over when he comes in. You know you have to turn it up a notch if you want to have a chance. That, or you have to hope his cutter cuts so much that he walks us or hits us.

JOHNNY DAMON, DISCUSSING MARIANO RIVERA

The most amazing thing is Mo's demeanor; not too many people have what he has. He's never intimidated, he'll challenge anyone, and you can't tell from his expression whether he was successful the night before or if he failed the night before. You have to have that in the role he has and, more importantly, where he's playing.

DEREK JETER

It's certainly an honor, but with that honor comes the responsibility to fulfill the contract.

HIDEKI MATSUI, AFTER SIGNING A NEW CONTRACT

The Yankees had their reasons for not wanting me to play. Major League Baseball had its reasons for wanting me to play. But at the end of the day, what was important to me is to win a championship ring with the Yankees.

HIDEKI MATSUI, ON HIS DECISION TO NOT PLAY FOR JAPAN IN THE WORLD BASEBALL CLASSIC

I don't want to be the wheel that's falling off the wagon here. That's where I am at right now. I want to feel like I am contributing.

RANDY JOHNSON, DESCRIBING HIS STRUGGLES DURING THE 2006 SEASON

On the day that I pitch, I expect us to win.

RANDY JOHNSON

Whatever it takes to win a championship. It's not about egos.

GARY SHEFFIELD

It's like trying to hit a bowling ball. The sinker that he throws is so heavy and it moves so late, the guys just beat it in the ground.

RON GUIDRY, DESCRIBING CHIEN-MING WANG

Chien-Ming Wang has overtaken Randy Johnson and Mike Mussina to become the New York Yankees' ace.

RONALD BLUM

He reminds me a lot of Roberto Alomar in terms of having the most fluid, pure swing of guys I've played with.

JIM THOME, DESCRIBING BOBBY ABREU

When I got to the plate, I never even imagined I would receive such an ovation. I felt nothing but appreciation.

BOBBY ABREU, DESCRIBING THE YANKEES FANS

Yankees Trivia

Alex Rodriguez was born in New York City on July 27, 1975.

It's obvious to everyone he's a special player. The thing that impresses me most is his maturity on the field.

CAL RIPKEN, DESCRIBING ALEX RODRIGUEZ

The sky's the limit with Alex. He is a natural.

KEN GRIFFEY, JR.

He learned in one or two years what it took me ten years to learn. He uses the whole field, foul line to foul line.

EDGAR MARTINEZ, ON A-ROD

I'm Alex's biggest fan. I brag on him so much that my teammates are sick of me talking about him.

DEREK JETER

The most impressive part of his defensive game is he has a very accurate arm and very good feet; he's very fleet-footed. He has a nose for the baseball, and that's a gift you can't teach. He's always had great range—phenomenal range—and he's always trying to be at the top of his game.

ALEX RODRIGUEZ, DESCRIBING DEREK JETER

We want to kill each other. I think we both drive each other and motivate each other. But, when we're off the field, we're like family. I think the nice thing about it is we became good friends before we even made it to the big leagues. That makes it more of a healthy relationship.

ALEX RODRIGUEZ, DISCUSSING HIS RELATIONSHIP WITH DEREK JETER

Our fans don't want to see us win the Wild Card. They want to see us win the division.

DEREK JETER

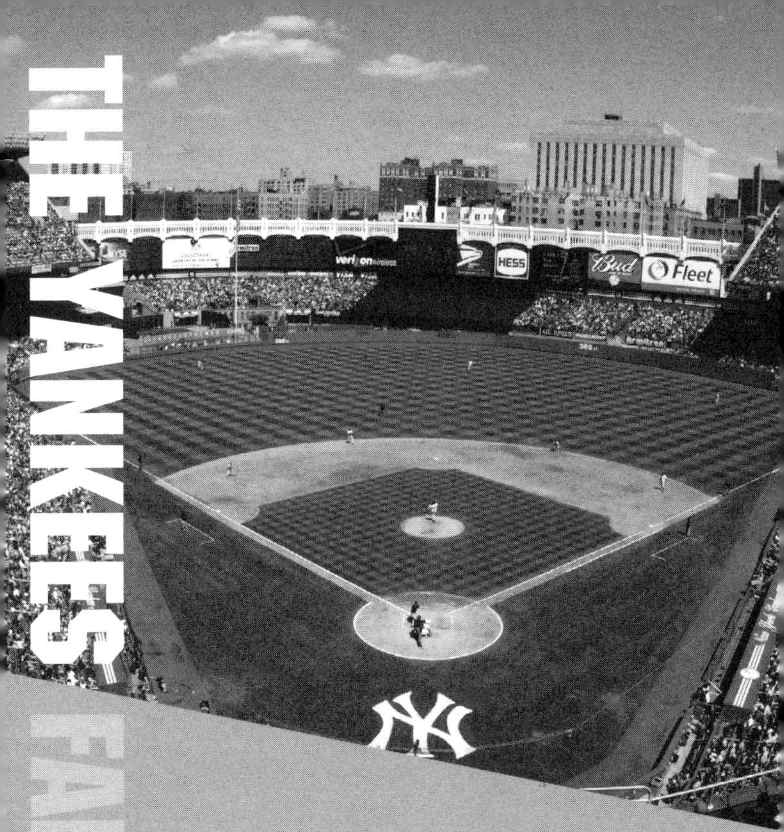

YANKEES MANAGEMENT

Yankees Trivia

Joe Torre has the longest tenure of any Yankees manager since Casey Stengel held the job for twelve straight years.

Throughout this modern era, Joe Torre has been at the helm. He is the latest in a long line of beleaguered Yankees managers but is enjoying one of the greatest runs of any to have held the job. There have been the ups—1996, 1998, 1999, and 2000—and there are always the downs. There are the losses in the postseason and the headaches that come with the day-to-day minutiae of the job. There is the pressure of New York and of working for The Boss. Big-name players need to be reigned in. Losing streaks have to be stopped so that the media can set their sights on the queens in Queens. Fan support makes for restful nights, but talk show rants can lead to incipient insomnia. Torre isn't the first to go through this, though. Just as each present-day player is standing on the shoulders of giants, so too is Joe Torre.

Several Yankees managers achieved fame on a par with the players. Some earned stardom for their managing while others earned it first on the field and then in the dugout. The Boss seems to prefer the latter. Torre was a good hitting catcher—not quite as good as Yogi, but good enough to not be embarrassed by his stats (MVP in 1971) if he is inducted into the Hall of Fame. Sweet Lou Piniella is another guy who knew how to play before figuring out the *X*s and *O*s of managing. Billy Martin was quotable and a bit wild, but also continued his winning ways . . . despite being fired nine hundred times! Look farther into the past and we find Casey Stengel who was even more quotable than Martin and a better manager, too. He successfully filled the shoes of the other man who deserves to be called "greatest Yankee manager," Joe McCarthy. Torre is chasing both of them for that title and although it might be hard for us modern-day fans to believe, there's a good chance that no one will ever surpass McCarthy and Stengel. They each won seven World Series championships and McCarthy's .614 regular season winning percentage still stands as a record.

And if you think Torre has it tough with today's egos, McCarthy came over from the Cubs to manage a team that was supposed to be Babe Ruth's to lead. Needless to say, when he found out he wasn't slated to be the manager, the Babe didn't give McCarthy a warm reception. These are the kinds of headaches that Yankees management has always had to deal with. By the way, McCarthy still led the Yanks to a championship that year, sticking it to his former team and becoming the first manager to win the World Series in both leagues. That's some good stuff, right there!

And you know, it's easy for the Yankee haters to say that the team's managers have it easy. What's so hard about filling out a lineup card when you've got all all-stars? Well, what's hard is keeping everyone happy. What's hard is playing the hot hand when they're all relatively hot. What's hard is keeping egos in check, from bat boys to The Boss. What's hard is playing below expectations in April and not losing your cool when you hear the blade of the guillotine being raised before the all-star break. What's hard is not winning the World Series when everyone from Vegas to Tampa has made your team the odds-on favorite. Fortunately, many of the Yankees managers have disappointed those who chose to bet against them.

Yankees Trivia

During his tenure as Yankees manager, Joe Torre has established a tradition. On the last day of the regular season, if the Yankees have clinched a playoff berth (which they've done every year under his leadership), Torre will choose one veteran to manage the team, one to act as pitching coach, and a third to act as hitting instructor. In 2006, Bernie managed, Moose handled the pitchers, and A-Rod talked hitting. Fun.

Joe McCarthy's Ten Commandments for Success in Baseball, as featured in the *Boston Herald* (1949)

1. Nobody ever became a ballplayer by walking after a ball.
2. You will never become a .300 hitter unless you take the bat off your shoulder.
3. An outfielder who throws in back of a runner is locking the barn after the horse is stolen.
4. Keep your head up and you may not have to keep it down.
5. When you start to slide, slide. He who changes his mind may have to change a good leg for a bad one.
6. Do not alibi on bad hops. Anybody can field the good ones.
7. Always run them out. You never can tell.
8. Do not quit.
9. Do not fight too much with the umpires. You cannot expect them to be as perfect as you are.
10. A pitcher who hasn't control hasn't anything.

The kid is the greatest proof of reincarnation. Nobody could get that stupid in one lifetime.

JOE MCCARTHY, DISCUSSING A PLAYER WHO WAS CAUGHT TRYING TO STEAL HOME

Give a boy a bat and a ball and a place to play, and you'll have a good citizen.

JOE MCCARTHY

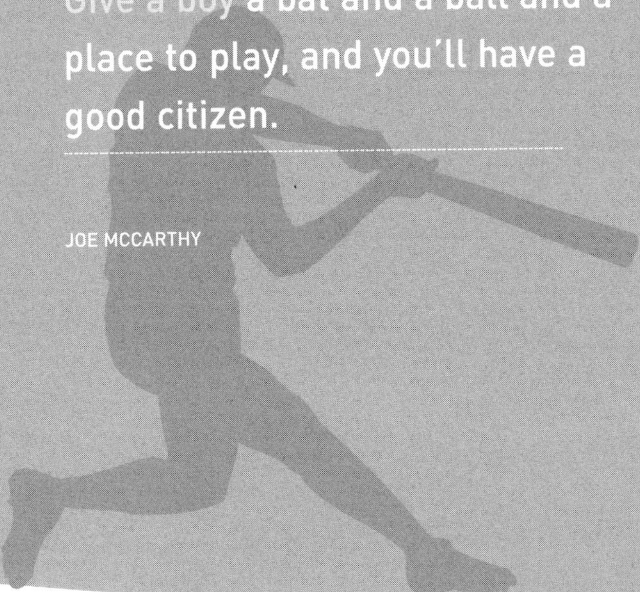

I'll never know.

JOE MCCARTHY, WHEN ASKED BY A REPORTER IF JOE DIMAGGIO COULD BUNT

Never a day went by when you didn't learn something from McCarthy.

JOE DIMAGGIO

Yankees Stats

Both Joe McCarthy and Casey Stengel hold the record for World Series championships with seven.

I've known all along that we had a great ball club. Now I guess everybody will have to admit it.

MILLER HUGGINS

You're first or you're nothing.

GEORGE WEISS, YANKEES GENERAL MANAGER AND HEAD OF THE FARM SYSTEM

The Yankees don't pay me to win every day, just two out of three.

CASEY STENGEL

See that fella over there? He's 20 years old. In 10 years, he's got a chance to be a star. Now that fella over there, he's 20 years old, too. In 10 years he's got a chance to be 30.

CASEY STENGEL

Now there's three things you can do in a baseball game: You can win or you can lose or it can rain.

CASEY STENGEL

Managing is getting paid for home runs that someone else hits.

CASEY STENGEL

I think it's a good idea.

CASEY STENGEL, WHEN ASKED BY A REPORTER AFTER A LOSS WHAT HE THOUGHT OF HIS TEAM'S EXECUTION

There's nobody on my ball club that doesn't go from first to third on a base hit, or from second to home. Every time you steal a base, you're taking a gamble on getting thrown out, and taking the bat out of the hitter's hand.

CASEY STENGEL

Sure I played, did you think I was born at the age of 70 sitting in a dugout trying to manage guys like you?

CASEY STENGEL, WHEN ASKED BY MICKEY MANTLE IF HE'D EVER PLAYED BALL

He was a great manager and had a great sense of character. He is right up there with Judge Landis, Babe Ruth, and Ty Cobb when it comes to baseball greatness.

TED WILLIAMS, DESCRIBING CASEY STENGEL

Casey knew his baseball. He only made it look like he was fooling around. He knew every move that was ever invented and some that we haven't even caught on to yet.

SPARKY ANDERSON, REMINISCING ABOUT CASEY STENGEL

It is fashionable to say that successful people, in any field, could have been whatever they wanted, but you could not picture Casey Stengel being anything else but what he was, the greatest showman baseball ever knew.

MICKEY HERSKOWITZ

I never saw a man who juggled his lineup so much and who played so many hunches so successfully.

CONNIE MACK, DESCRIBING CASEY STENGEL

There is no such thing as second place.

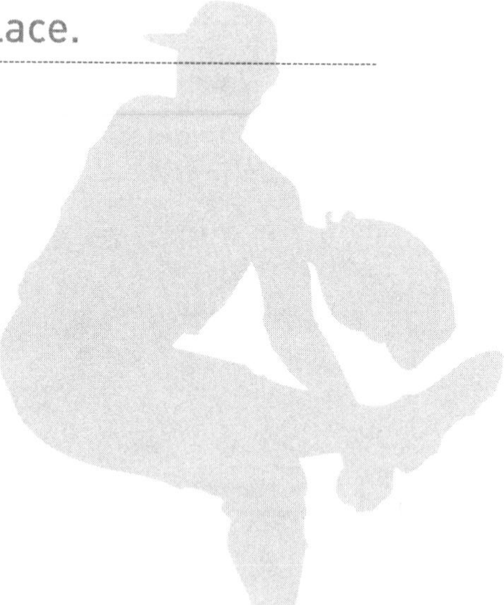

GABE PAUL

A good ball club.

YOGI BERRA, WHEN ASKED WHAT MAKES A MANAGER GOOD

Playing for Yogi is like playing for your father; playing for Billy is like playing for your father-in-law.

DON BAYLOR, COMPARING YOGI BERRA AND BILLY MARTIN

All I know is, I pass people on the street these days, and they don't know whether to say hello or to say good-bye.

BILLY MARTIN

Everything looks nicer when you win. The girls are prettier. The cigars taste better. The trees are greener.

BILLY MARTIN

Everybody judges players different. I judge a player by what he does for his ball club and not by what he does for himself. I think the name of the game is self-sacrifice.

BILLY MARTIN

What does George know about Yankee pride? When did he ever play for the Yankees?

BILLY MARTIN

One hundred ten thousand ears in this ballpark, and he's got to hit my ear.

DON ZIMMER, AFTER BEING HIT IN THE HEAD BY A FOUL BALL DURING THE 1999 AMERICAN LEAGUE DIVISION SERIES

That's the thing about the Yankees. They bring it every night. They want to win. They have a passion to win. That's good.

LARRY BOWA

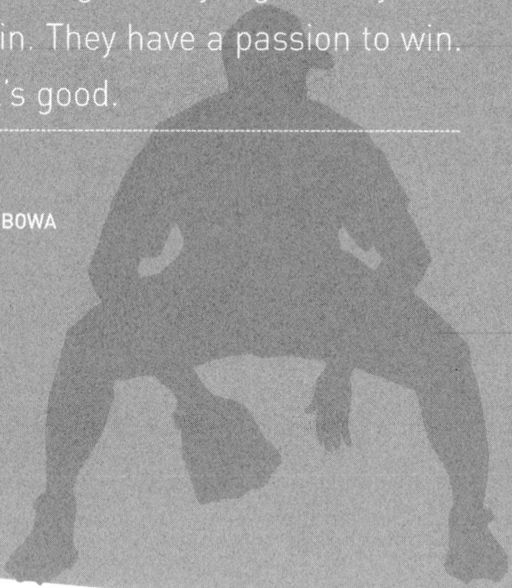

Yankees Trivia

Joe Torre is a hero on and off the field. His Safe at Home Foundation has raised funds and brought national attention to the issue of domestic abuse, especially as it affects children.

I don't think anybody can question the chemistry, class, and ruggedness of this team.

JOE TORRE, AFTER THE YANKEES DEFEATED THE ORIOLES IN THE 1996 AMERICAN LEAGUE CHAMPIONSHIP SERIES

We just feel as a team that we know what our capabilities are. We don't try and go outside of ourselves. I think that's very important, that we just think in small bits and bites. Because that's what we need to do.

JOE TORRE

We realized that in spite of all the sadness and devastation, people were looking to us for . . . I wouldn't say relief, but a distraction, a support system. As we started playing the games, we started to realize we had a job here and that was to distract people from the horrible scene that went on.

JOE TORRE, REFERRING TO THE GAMES THE YANKEES PLAYED FOLLOWING 9/11

Winning is a lot of fun. I remember having a meeting a couple years ago and telling the guys: "You're not enjoying yourselves." O'Neill said to me afterwards, "Skip, it's not fun unless you win."

JOE TORRE

I feel emptiness, and he probably won't be able to close his eyes for two or three days.

JOE TORRE, SPEAKING OF MARLINS MANAGER JACK MCKEON AFTER LOSING THE 2003 WORLD SERIES

Here we go again.

JOE TORRE, BEFORE ANOTHER SERIES AGAINST THE RED SOX

Yankees Trivia

Four men have managed both the Yankees and the Mets: Joe Torre, Casey Stengel, Yogi Berra, and Dallas Green.

I'm just pleased I'm able to stay on and do this.

JOE TORRE, AFTER RECEIVING WORD FROM GEORGE STEINBRENNER THAT HE WOULD BE MANAGER AGAIN IN 2007

THE BOSS

George Steinbrenner is *the* modern-day Yankee. Having owned the team since 1973, he has twice gone through stretches of the best of times and twice gone through stretches of the worst of times. Although he might not be as hotheaded as in younger days, he's still driven by one desire and one desire alone: to win.

Given the fact that The Boss was born and raised in the cradle of American football (Ohio) it should be no surprise that every game is important to him. One NFL game is worth ten baseball games, after all. But above and beyond the math, what irks The Boss more than anything is the simple fact of losing. He didn't win. We didn't win. And we should've won. We could've won. We didn't. Steinbrenner finds losses to be costly and embarrassing. Some might say it's stupid for him to invest his money in a player and then ruin that investment as he did when he called Hideki Irabu a "fat toad," but you know what? It is Steinbrenner's cash-given right to be upset when he sees that his investment is too lazy to cover first base. The

Boss pays a lot to bring the best available players into The Bronx and that's why when I invest my money to go see a Yankees game I feel good because I know I'm not going to get cheated. And if I do, if somebody in pinstripes doesn't give his all, The Boss is going to be twice as ticked off about it as I am.

If I was a fan of another team, I might question where my money is going. Toward that young secretary's year-end bonus? Toward the owner's new yacht? Toward the GM's time-share in the Caribbean? But not if you're a fan of the Yankees. Bleacher Creatures pay four times as much today as they did fifteen years ago, but at least they know that the money they're spending will be put back into the team. All of the money that comes from the tickets and the merchandise, as well as all of the money generated by YES, goes toward the talent (after subtracting for revenue sharing, of course). This is why other teams love the Yankees and why their fans should, too. The Yankees put people in the stands when they come to town and every year they buy each team an additional middle reliever or role player (if that's what their management chooses to do with the money). Steinbrenner pads the pockets of these other owners and then has to listen to them complain when he signs another free agent. No wonder he takes such pleasure from beating everyone. It's that football mentality.

From 1903 to 1915, Frank Ferrell and Bill Devery owned the Yankees, although the team was called the Highlanders back then. They bought the team for $18,000 and moved them from Baltimore to New York. Then the colonels came along. Colonel Jacob Ruppert and Colonel Tillinghast L'Hommedieu Huston purchased the team for $460,000 and owned it in tandem for seven years. They put pinstripes on the players' uniforms, stole Babe Ruth from Boston, and began construction on Yankee Stadium. Not a bad run! As *Time* magazine, October 10, 1932, described Ruppert, who bought out Huston's share in 1922:

Fourth Game, Colonel Jacob Ruppert, the 65-year-old bon vivant who owns the Yankees, cannot bear his team to lose, cannot bear to watch a close game, let alone a close World Series. Even to win in four straight games is too close for him until the fourth game is won. He begged his men to win last Sunday and end his terrible suspense. The Yankees obliged with all the trimmings.

What they did was win the 1932 World Series. The colonel was pleased!

In 1945, Dan Topping and Del Webb bought the team for $2.8 million and enjoyed possibly the finest run in team history. In 1964, they sold 80 percent of the team to CBS for $11.2 million. CBS bought the remaining 20 percent then sold the team, at a loss, to a Steinbrenner-led group that paid just $10.3 million. Catfish Hunter was signed as the league's first big-money free agent, Reggie Jackson followed Catfish's lead, migrating east from Oakland, and the rest, as they say, is history.

But before calling it history, I'd like to point out one last detail about the savvy of our Boss. According to the September 28, 1998 *Business Week* article "The Yankees: Steinbrenner's Money Machine," Steinbrenner was part of an investment group that put up $6 million and borrowed the other $4.3 million. And you know how much Steinbrenner chipped in? Out of that $6 million, only $168,000 was his! Then, he bought out the other partners. He put his stamp on the team. Despite the bumps in the road of the 1980s and early 1990s, he put his money into building the team up. Smoothing out the road, if you will. Paving the way to greatness. The proof is there, too. Between 1978 and 1990, the team didn't show any sort of a profit—including a $31 million loss in 1990—and since then, they've been just slightly in the black. Even the brains at *Business Week* can see what Steinbrenner likes to invest in: winning.

Yankees Trivia

The Boss was born on July 4, 1930.

I don't say I'm St. George.

GEORGE STEINBRENNER

He fires people like it's a bodily function!

GEORGE COSTANZA, DESCRIBING STEINBRENNER ON *SEINFELD*

Look, I'm not saying that I'm a calm, peaceful guy. I'm not Marian the Librarian. I'm a hard-driving guy, and sometimes I get upset.

GEORGE STEINBRENNER

Owning the Yankees is like owning the Mona Lisa.

GEORGE STEINBRENNER

Yankee Stadium Stats

In 1972, the final year of CBS ownership, attendance at The Stadium was less than one million, but in 2006 the Yankees drew more than four million fans.

It was the class and dignity which he led his life that made him part of all of us. I will forever treasure the close friendship we shared over the years.

GEORGE STEINBRENNER, DISCUSSING HIS FRIENDSHIP WITH JOE DIMAGGIO

He says all the right things, like it's Jeter's team. I want to correct him on that—it's my team.

GEORGE STEINBRENNER, DESCRIBING JASON GIAMBI WHEN HE SIGNED WITH THE YANKEES

There is an old Scottish proverb that says, "I am wounded but I am not slain. I shall lay me down and bleed a while, then I shall rise and fight again." That should be the feeling of all of the Yankees.

GEORGE STEINBRENNER, AFTER LOSING THE AMERICAN LEAGUE DIVISION SERIES IN 2002

I haven't always done a good job, and I haven't always been successful—but I know that I have tried.

GEORGE STEINBRENNER

I think that a hands-on approach is very important. You have to know your ballplayers, and who has the ability and the intense hunger and drive to win.

GEORGE STEINBRENNER

Steinbrenner himself was 50% owner, 50% fan and 100% businessman. That totals 200%, which is both shaky mathematics and perhaps another indication that George is larger than life.

ROGER KAHN, DESCRIBING THE BOSS IN HIS BOOK
OCTOBER MEN

I was at the game with him during the 2004 ALDS and I got up to go to the bathroom. He looked at me and said "No! Don't go to the bathroom until they win the World Series!" and I haven't gone to the bathroom since. P.S. To the Yankees: can you hurry up? I'm dying here!

REGIS PHILBIN, ON WATCHING A YANKEES PLAYOFF GAME WITH THE BOSS

It's a good thing Babe Ruth isn't still here—George would have him bat seventh and say he's overweight.

GRAIG NETTLES

There is nothing quite so limited as being a limited partner of George Steinbrenner's.

JOHN MCMULLEN

With all my years with the Mets and the Cardinals, I'd never worked for an owner that was so committed to winning and putting the best possible players on the field.

JOE TORRE

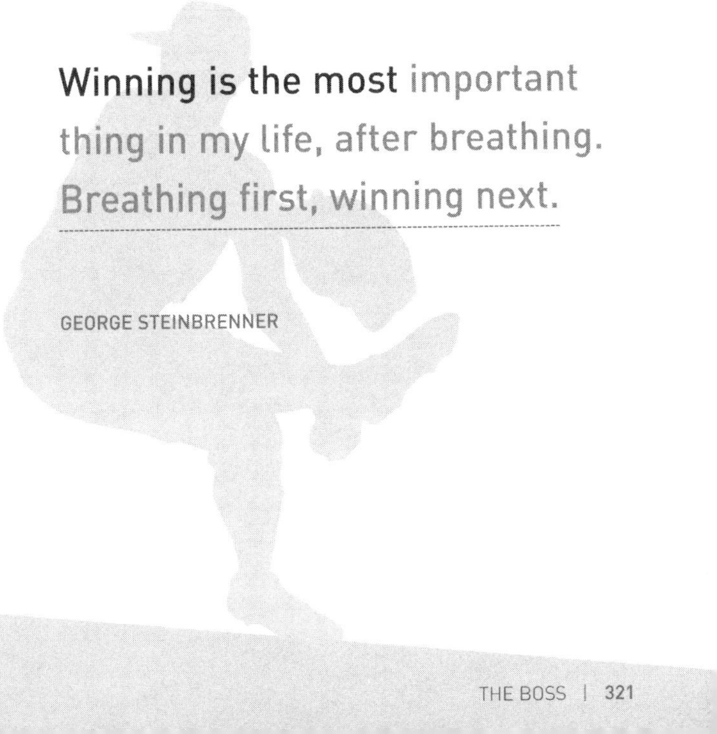

Winning is the most important thing in my life, after breathing. Breathing first, winning next.

GEORGE STEINBRENNER

BEING THERE: FROM THE BLEACHER CREATURES TO THE STADIUM ITSELF

Yankees Trivia

Jacob Ruppert decided to build Yankee Stadium when he was told the Yankees could no longer play at the Polo Grounds, which they were leasing from the New York baseball Giants (they were outdrawing the Giants!). So, Ruppert had The Stadium built right across the Harlem River from the Polo Grounds.

For most of my life, I've approached Yankee Stadium from the north, driving down the Saw Mill River Parkway to the New York State Thruway, which becomes the Major Deegan Expressway once you cross into The Bronx. To my right is the Harlem River, sparkling in the sunlight. To my left is always some sort of dented SUV with Jersey plates, filled with screaming guys who always act this way, let alone after a few road sodas. These are my Yankees brothers! As Exit 6 draws near, I let them pull in front and they give an appreciative fist pump followed by the affectionate cry of "Let's go, Yankees!" Clap! Clap! Clapclapclap!!! Our caravan of pinstripe pride leaves the Deegan and dips down toward Lot 13B: VIP parking to the right, riffraff to the left. I follow the Jersey boys to the left.

If I'd stayed on the Deegan, Yankee Stadium would've come into view with the Louisville Slugger bat in the forefront and the little message board atop The House That Ruth Built to advertise the start time of that day's game. There's always a thank-you message when the season ends and another kind of message once Times Square shakes off its New Year's hangover: the countdown to Opening Day. But entering the Kinney Parking Lot, the only view I'm offered is of tailgaters, scalpers, and T-shirt hawks. I pay and park and then I'm walking across the overheated tunnel that spans the Metro North train line, the same flute player as always taking requests for songs like "Popeye," "The Flintstones," and "Yankee Doodle Dandy."

If first pitch is 1:05, I emerge from the tunnel no later than noon. According to the gridlocksam.com Web site, "If you're driving, leave early, very early. If you arrive in the area 45 minutes before game time, you'll probably miss the first inning." I don't want to miss the first inning. I don't even want to miss Robert Merrill's recorded rendition of the National Anthem! That being said, I like to quench my thirst in the style of the Jersey boys and once inside the beers will run me $7, so I move away from the bat and ticket booth and turn left on River Avenue where I'm greeted by a timeless city scene. Light may sparkle on the Harlem River, but it dapples here beneath the elevated subway. This is the land of bars and bodegas, souvenir shops, and even a bowling alley: This is where Stan's Sports Bar & Restaurant is. If you like heavy metal music and cold beer, there is no other place for a Yankees pregame. Across the street, I watch the line for the bleachers form behind blue NYPD barricades. Whoever I'm going to the game with also watches in silent appreciation. You can't really talk in Stan's—Axl Rose won't allow it. Even the subway, rumbling overhead, is drowned out. "You know where you are? You're in the jungle, baby." And then the warning to the opposing team: "You're gonna diiiiie!"

I spot the Jersey boys. They're brown-bagging it as they wait to go inside and take a seat among their fellow Bleacher Creatures. Soon enough, they'll be shouting "Let's go, Yankees!" Clap! Clap! Clapclapclap!!! Then, they'll greet each of the starting Yankees, chanting the player's name until acknowledged with a wave. The cops don't give their brown bags a second look. I finish my beer and head for the door. It's game time.

Tickets don't get ripped anymore, they get scanned. But that's OK. The guys working the turnstiles are one hundred years old and I know they actually saw the great Yankees in their heyday. If you haven't figured it out yet, I'm taking you through this, step by step, because whether you've been or have not been it's fun to get lost in a game day for a few minutes. Am I right? And for those of you who haven't been to The Stadium, make sure to go inside even earlier so that you can tour Monument Park. There you'll find those Yankees greats that the ticket scanners once cheered for. The past comes alive in Monument Park and only the opposition need fear these ghosts.

I walk up the runway and my eyes drop from the blue sky to the Bronx County Courthouse to the facade of The Stadium to the green, green grass cut in Quaker quilt patterns. Behind home plate is the press box with the banners for CBS and YES hanging and where as a boy I would search for Phil Rizzuto's face above the WPIX sign. For the big games, an ESPN banner or, better yet, a FOX banner is displayed. FOX means I'm there for a playoff game! In 2003, my wife and I rode the train down with way too many blindly optimistic, big-mouthed Red Sox fans, then laughed all the way home as they buried their heads in their hands. Game Seven had a FOX banner hanging up, that's for sure. I sit down and share the one-nod greeting with my neighbors. The music kicks in as the Yankees take the field. I stand for the National Anthem and remove my cap just as all my heroes do the same. Robert Merrill finishes, Derek Jeter returns his cap to its rightful place, the umpire yells, "Play ball!" and the Bleacher Creatures begin their roll call. This is the home of champions. This is Yankee Stadium.

I believe in ghosts. And we've got some ghosts in this stadium.

DEREK JETER, AFTER THE GAME SEVEN AMERICAN LEAGUE CHAMPIONSHIP SERIES VICTORY OVER THE RED SOX IN 2003

Yankees Trivia

Before 1903, the Yankees actually played in Baltimore and were known as the Orioles. Upon moving to New York, they became the Highlanders and in 1913, when sports writers complained that "Highlanders" was too long for headlines, the team changed its name to the Yankees.

When on opening day of 1923, Fred Lieb of the *New York World* baptized the stadium, "The House That Ruth Built," he foresaw the reciprocal grandeur between the Babe and Yankee Stadium that would enlarge the reputations of both ballplayer and ballpark and endure beyond the Babe's death and the stadium's renovation.

PETER CARINO

Some yard.

BABE RUTH, AFTER SEEING YANKEE STADIUM FOR THE FIRST TIME

It is the most magical ballpark ever built. Playing there as a Yankee was like being in the Marines, feeling that you were in a special ballpark, special town, special uniform, special history.

PHIL LINZ

To play 18 years in Yankee Stadium is the best thing that could ever happen to a ballplayer.

MICKEY MANTLE

The crack of a bat sounded amplified in cavernous Yankee Stadium, sprinkled lightly with fans on a cool September evening.

WILLIAM E. GEIST

Yankee Stadium was made for rabbits and giants. You have to be a rabbit to catch a ball out there in the outfield and you have to be a giant to hit the ball out.

CARLTON FISK

That's the nicest thing a returning player could ever ask for. It shows how classy the New York fans are. It gave me a warm feeling inside.

WADE BOGGS, ON THE OVATION HE RECEIVED DURING HIS FIRST RETURN TO YANKEE STADIUM

To pitch a perfect game wearing pinstripes at Yankee Stadium, it's unbelievable. Growing up a Yankee fan, to come out here and make history, it really is a dream come true.

DAVID WELLS

Yankee Stadium Stats

The dimensions of Yankee Stadium are as follows: leftfield line, 318 feet; rightfield line, 314 feet; and center field, 408 feet.

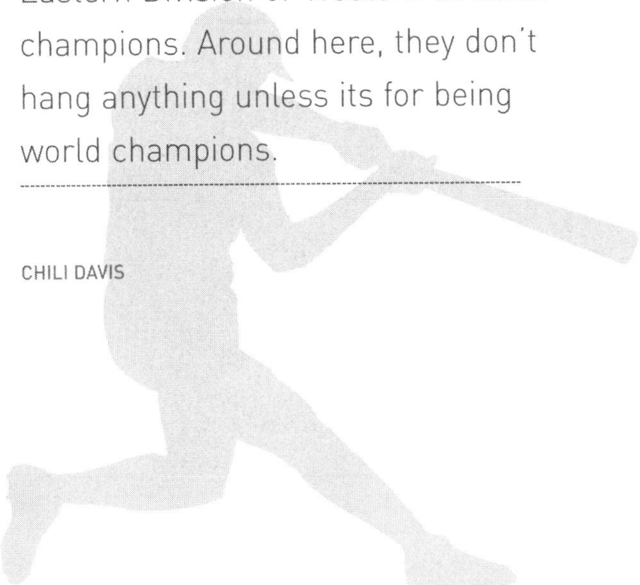

When you go to other parks, they hang banners for the wild-card or Eastern Division or Western Division champions. Around here, they don't hang anything unless its for being world champions.

CHILI DAVIS

My office is at Yankee stadium. Yes, dreams do come true.

DEREK JETER

Yankee Stadium is my favorite stadium; I'm not going to lie to you. There's a certain feel you get in Yankee Stadium.

DEREK JETER

You're always surprised. You never know what's gonna happen at Yankee Stadium.

BERNIE WILLIAMS, ON THE BLEACHER CREATURE ROLL CALL

I've always said that's the ultimate place to play baseball. It's the sports capital of the world. It doesn't get any better than that.

JASON GIAMBI

You know it as soon as you walk in Yankee Stadium. The electricity is there every time, every day.

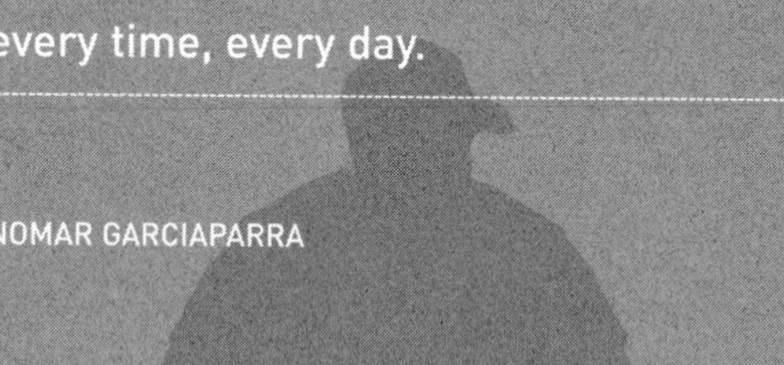

NOMAR GARCIAPARRA

Yankees Trivia

If you're looking for the official scorecard when watching a game at Yankee Stadium, it can be found in the *Yankees Magazine*

Very few buildings managed to meld their history literally with the present. Yankee Stadium does. There is something glorious about knowing that the physical form of the structure (never mind how badly it has been altered) ties Derek Jeter to Joe DiMaggio.

PAUL GOLDBERGER, *NEW YORK TIMES* ARCHITECTURE CRITIC

When I became manager here, the first time I walked down the runway leading to the dugout from the clubhouse I thought of Ruth, Gehrig, DiMaggio and all the others taking the same path. That's what The Stadium is all about.

JOE TORRE

Attention Fans, Welcome to NOVEMBER BASEBALL

YANKEE STADIUM SCOREBOARD ON NOVEMBER 1, 2001

Yankees Trivia

Bob Sheppard is famous in New York for being the public address announcer for both the Yankees and the NFL's Giants.

Most guys won't admit it, but it can be an intimidating thing your first few times there. All the lore of the stadium and the mystique can be difficult to deal with.

AL LEITER

Aura and Mystique are dancers in a nightclub.

CURT SCHILLING, WHEN ASKED ABOUT THE AURA AND MYSTIQUE OF YANKEE STADIUM

But the real New York can be found in right field of the Yankee Stadium bleachers.

WILL LEITCH

Yankee Stadium is the grandest of all the old-time great parks.

ALEX BELTH, *SPORTS ILLUSTRATED*, APRIL 27, 2006

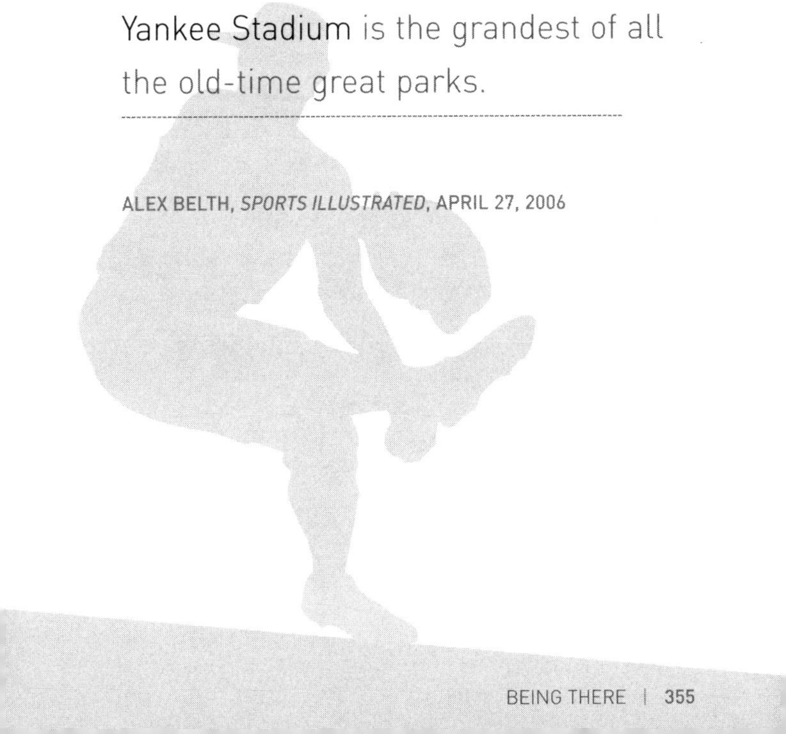

Yankee Stadium is an iconic stadium, a place where Ruth and Gehrig played, where popes and presidents have spoken. But so, too, will the new Yankee Stadium be an iconic stadium.

GEORGE PATAKI, AT THE GROUNDBREAKING CEREMONY FOR THE NEW YANKEE STADIUM

Yankee Stadium is an American monument that has endured for 84 years. Today we are breaking ground on a new Yankee Stadium, a new monument and new memories for the coming generations of fans.

BUD SELIG, AT THE SAME CEREMONY

Note: This chapter is written in reference to the Yankee Stadium at East 161st Street and River Avenue. In August 2006, the Yankees broke ground on a new stadium. It will seat 53,000 fans, which is 4,000 fewer than the old stadium. There will be more luxury boxes, plus state-of-the-art restaurants, bars, and shops, and all told the complex will cost more than $1 billion. Neil DeMause of BaseballProspectus.com writes,

The outside is going to look like Yankee Stadium in 1923 on steroids. That's the shell. In between the facade and the seating bowl will be an enormous shopping concourse. That's what the Yankees are really after. When they say they can't renovate the current stadium, they are talking about concessions stands and restaurants. The attempt is to bring all the money that Yankees fans are spending into Yankee Stadium. The intent is to take away business that fans would spend on the street outside the stadium. I'm sure they'll have some locals run some stands in the new park, but they'll pay serious rent to the Yankees.

If you're looking for me, I'll be at Stan's with Axl and the Jersey boys.

THE MEDIA, FICTION, FAMOUS FOLKS, AND EVEN FREDDY SEZ

Is this baseball or Entertainment Tonight?

TIM RAINES, DESCRIBING THE MEDIA IN NEW YORK

No team in professional sports has been portrayed more often, in stories both fictional and true, than our beloved Yankees. Unfortunately, they are the perfect tool for anyone hoping to earn sympathy votes from the audience. In *Damn Yankees*, a member of the Washington Senators is even willing to sign a deal with the devil to beat our boys. When Kevin Costner lugs his wearied body onto the hill for one last game, his opponent, of course, is the

Yankees. *For Love of the Game* and for hate of the Yankees! Major League used the Yankees as the icing on the cake when the Tom Berenger-led Indians were completing their improbable season. Ernest Hemingway knew better, though, and in *The Old Man and the Sea*, his aging hero, Santiago, taught his son to respect the Yankees.

Famous people talk about the Yankees all the time, too. They have a career-related need to be associated with All Things A-List, so they appear whenever the cameras are rolling! All except Ben Affleck and Matt Damon who showed their devotion to the Red Sox in *Good Will Hunting*. They got to celebrate the World Series win in 2004, but that's one in their lifetime compared to the six I've enjoyed. Hey, Matt, how do you like them apples?

Finally, there's the media. They go any way the wind blows, trying to sell as many papers or draw in as many viewers as possible. And I find no fault with that. In a way, they're no different from us Yankees fanatics. I'm not one to boo, but I can certainly envision my New Jersey brethren laying into a player when he isn't bringing the goods. But redemption is always one good at bat or outing away and Yankees fans are always willing to let a player back into their hearts and sing his praises. We've all come to expect that the back pages will scream the same, good and bad.

Rather than talk about the media in general, I'd prefer to pay homage to the homers: the broadcasters who deliver the games to us through the radio or on the boob tube. First and foremost is the Hall of Famer known as the "Voice of the Yankees," Mel Allen. Then there's the voice of my youth, the tall tales and all, the Scooter himself, Philip Francis Rizzuto. He was like the grandfather I never had, chortling on about cannoli and golf outings and how he hoped to beat the traffic over the bridge. Tom Seaver and Bill White played straight men to Rizzuto's rampant silliness and it was a pleasure to behold. Let's not disrespect Rizzuto's on-field accomplishments, either. Sure, the cow the Yanks gave him on Phil Rizzuto Day was able to knock him on his rear, but the Scooter was the American League MVP in 1950 and owns seven, count 'em, seven World Series championship rings. Rizzuto represents my roots while John Sterling and Michael Kay represent my modern-day memories. I loved them on the radio and still wish that Michael Kay hadn't switched over to YES, but I get what I need. When Kay was partnered with Jim Kaat and Ken Singleton there was no better booth in baseball. I still miss Kaat's insight and self-effacing humor. Paul O'Neill, Al Leiter, and John Flaherty are doing a decent job filling the gap, though. David "Uzi" Justice also brings quite a bit to the table when paired with Bob Lorenz behind the desk in the YES studios. I used to be hesitant about mixing in all of these former players, but I'm enjoying it more and more. The broadcasts are tight and the recently retired do have something to offer. I hate to say it, but quite a bit more to offer than that favorite from my youth.

Although YES has scored quite a few Emmys, the majority of my games come via the radio. Even without Kay by his side, and even with the need for a stronger eyeglasses prescription, John Sterling's enthusiasm definitely adds to the games. And, it goes without saying, to the end of the game. There is no happier moment than when he lets rip his signature, "The Yankees win. Theeeee Yankees win!" I can live with hearing that 110 times a year, that's for sure.

Of note is the fact that in all of the baseball, hockey, and basketball games that Sterling has been scheduled to call, he hasn't missed an assignment since 1981. No calling in sick. No taking a vacation. Even when his wife had their triplets, he called every game. That's the kind of drive and dedication that The Boss likes.

If you need directions to home plate at Fenway Park, just stop and ask any New York Yankee. They've all been there already.

FROM THE *BOSTON GLOBE* AFTER THE RED SOX SURRENDERED THEIR 14.5 GAME LEAD IN 1978

Have faith in the Yankees, my son.

SANTIAGO TO HIS SON IN ERNEST HEMINGWAY'S *THE OLD MAN AND THE SEA*

The majority of American males put themselves to sleep by striking out the batting order of the New York Yankees.

JAMES THURBER

Where have you gone, Joe DiMaggio?
A nation turns its lonely eyes to you.

PAUL SIMON

After 19 years in the big leagues, 40-year-old Billy Chapel has trudged to the mound for over 4,000 innings. But tonight, he's pitching against time, he's pitching against the future, against age, against ending. Tonight, he will make the fateful walk to the loneliest spot in the world, the pitching mound at Yankee Stadium, to push the sun back into the sky and give us one more day of summer.

VIN SCULLY, IN *FOR LOVE OF THE GAME*

I read somewhere they're thinking of handicapping the Yankees . . . making them wear extra weight, like racehorses.

THE DEVIL IN *DAMN YANKEES*

Yankees Trivia

The following movies all involve, in some way, shape, or form, our beloved Yankees: *Damn Yankees, Pride of the Yankees, That Touch of Mink, For Love of the Game, 61**, *The Babe, The Babe Ruth Story, Nine Innings from Ground Zero, Safe at Home*, and *Everyone's Hero.*

He's a natural. Young. Handsome. He can play his ass off, playing shortstop for the Yankees. What more do you want? The fact that he's here in the greatest sports town—greatest city in the world—makes it that much better.

SPIKE LEE, DESCRIBING DEREK JETER

I love his work ethic. He has a great attitude. He has the qualities that separate superstars from everyday people, and a lot of it is attributable to his great family background.

MICHAEL JORDAN, DISCUSSING DEREK JETER

Mickey Mantle just was everything. At my Bar Mitzvah I had an Oklahoma accent.

BILLY CRYSTAL

Orlando Hernandez is a very lucky man. He escapes the dictatorial reign of a ruthless tyrant and ends up working for George Steinbrenner.

DAVID LETTERMAN

When I heard this CD, I was blown away by his talent. Go Bernie, it's a home run!

PAUL MCCARTNEY, COMMENTING ON BERNIE WILLIAMS'S CD, *THE JOURNEY WITHIN*

Every great team in baseball history will now be compared to these 1998 Yankees. And I predict, that when the game of baseball is finally done, this team will be remembered as the greatest team of all time.

RUDY GIULIANI

My kid was a great baseball player. I thought I had it made. Front-row seats at Yankee Stadium. Then he turned sixteen and wanted to be a rapper.

JAMES CAAN

Ty Cobb has ruled—and Ruth has sung his

tune—Tris Speaker was a melody in rime—

DiMaggio—you won't forget him soon—

Here is the master artist of our time.

GRANTLAND RICE, DESCRIBING JOE DIMAGGIO

There has never been anything like it. Even as these lines are batted out on the office typewriter, youths dash out of the AP and UP ticker room every two or three minutes shouting, "Ruth hit one! Gehrig just hit another one!"

PAUL GALLICO

The first team in history to have magicians, miracle men, jinns, a Beowulf and a couple of Thors on it. It is a team out of folklore and mythology.

H. I. PHILLIPS, WRITING ABOUT THE 1927 YANKEES IN THE *NEW YORK SUN*

The reason the Yankees never lay an egg is because they don't operate on chicken feed.

DAN PARKER

The essence of the Yankees is that they win. From in front or from behind, they win. And that's why the history of the New York Yankees is virtually the history of baseball.

DAVE ANDERSON

In a tough age which called for tough men in baseball, the Yankees were the toughest. They were managed by a perfectionist, bossed by a president who hated second place, and owned by a man who could say, even with a seventeen-game lead in 1936, "I can't stand the suspense. When are we going to clinch it?"

DAVID VOIGT

Interviewing Roger Clemens was like interviewing John Wayne from the Searchers. He has that kind of intensity. What you see on the mound is pretty much what you find in the locker room.

RICHARD LALLY

It's been said before, but it's true: for Red Sox fans, watching Clemens thrive as a Yankee is the equivalent of watching your ex-wife marry your sworn mortal enemy—then live happily ever after.

SEAN MCADAM

Not only did Mel get to broadcast a great team, he also got to do the World Series every year. He did 20 World Series in his broadcasting career. . . . Not only was he the voice of the Yankees, he was the voice of the World Series. Every fall, fans could set their clock by the voice of Mel Allen.

STEPHEN BORELLI

Mel made players like Joe DiMaggio, Yogi Berra and those great Yankee teams seem larger than life. He became just as famous in New York as any player. . . . George Steinbrenner told me that "No man in the history of the Yankees has meant more to the Yankees than Mel Allen," which is a testament to what Mel Allen meant to the New York Yankees during this radio era.

STEPHEN BORELLI

The rivalry is a big part of the fabric of the community in New England. But the rivalry is a bit one-sided.

DAN SHAUGHNESSY (AND HE DOESN'T MEAN ONE-SIDED IN FAVOR OF THE RED SOX!)

That one game surpasses any other one I've ever been connected with. Those two teams—and the whole season boiling down to one game at Fenway—it was quite a moment for everyone who was there or watched it on TV.

FRANK MESSER, DESCRIBING THE ONE-GAME PLAYOFF AGAINST THE RED SOX IN 1978

I'm glad I don't play anymore. I could never learn all those handshakes.

PHIL RIZZUTO

Yankees Trivia

In 1948, Mel Allen was the first announcer to say, "Going, going, gone!" after a home run.

Here's the pitch. Mantle swings. There's a tremendous drive going into deep left field! It's going, going! It's over the bleachers . . . over the sign atop the bleachers . . . into the yards of houses across the street! It's got to be one of the longest runs I've ever seen! How about that!

MEL ALLEN, DESCRIBING MICKEY MANTLE'S 565-FOOT HOME RUN AGAINST THE WASHINGTON SENATORS

Here comes Roger Maris, they're standing up, waiting to see if Roger is going to hit number sixty-one, here's the windup, the pitch to Roger, WAY outside, ball one. The fans are starting to boo, low, ball two. That one was in the dirt and the boos get louder. Two balls, no strikes on Roger Maris. Here's the windup, fastball, hit deep to right. This could be it. Waaay back there. Holy cow, he did it. Sixty-one home runs!

PHIL RIZZUTO

Deep to left! Yastrzemski will not get it!

BILL WHITE, CALLING BUCKY DENT'S THREE-RUN HOME RUN OFF THE RED SOX IN 1978'S ONE-GAME PLAYOFF

Chris Chambliss singled. Roy White singled. That's how the top of the seventh began for the Yankees. All was just foreshadowing for Earl Russell Dent out of Savannah, Georgia.

HARVEY FROMMER, DESCRIBING THE INNING WHEN BUCKY DENT HIT HIS HOME RUN

Yankees Trivia

In that infamous game, Reggie Jackson provided the insurance runs with his two-run home run after Bucky Dent's three-run home run.

David Wells has pitched a perfect game! 27 up, 27 down! Baseball immortality for David Wells.

JOHN STERLING

You cannot predict this game. It's impossible.

JOHN STERLING

Bern baby bern!

JOHN STERLING, CALLING ANOTHER ONE OF BERNIE WILLIAMS'S BIG HITS

Jorgie **juiced one!**

JOHN STERLING, CALLING A JORGE POSADA HOME RUN

And the crowd rises as one . . .

JOHN STERLING, WHENEVER THERE ARE TWO STRIKES AND TWO OUTS IN THE NINTH INNING

And the 3–2 pitch . . . Swung on and drilled deep to right! There it goes! That ball is gone! A grand slam into the upper deck for Tino Martinez! And the Yankees lead 9–5! Oh, what a home run for Tino Martinez!

MICHAEL KAY, DESCRIBING TINO MARTINEZ'S HOME RUN IN GAME ONE OF THE 1998 WORLD SERIES

Hit on the ground on a hop to Brosius, fields, throws across . . . in time! Ballgame over! World Series over! Yankees win! Theeeee Yankees Win!

JOHN STERLING, CALLING THE LAST OUT OF THE 1998 WORLD SERIES

From ear to ear, you can feel Darryl Strawberry smiling.

JOE BUCK, DURING THE 1998 WORLD SERIES WHEN STRAWBERRY WAS UNABLE TO PLAY AFTER BEING DIAGNOSED WITH COLON CANCER

Swung on and drilled to right field, going back Sanders, on the track, at the wall . . . See ya! A home run for Derek Jeter! He is Mr. November! Oh what a home run by Derek Jeter!

MICHAEL KAY, DESCRIBING DEREK JETER'S HOME RUN IN GAME FOUR OF THE 2001 WORLD SERIES

I have never seen anything like this.

TIM MCCARVER, AFTER SCOTT BROSIUS'S GAME FIVE HOME RUN IN THE 2001 WORLD SERIES (NO OTHER TEAM HAD ENJOYED TWO, TWO-RUN, GAME-TYING, NINTH-INNING HOME RUNS BEFORE)

FREDDY SEZ YANKS IN SEVEN, DON'T LOOK GLUM-CHUM.

FREDDY SEZ'S SIGN BEFORE GAME SEVEN AGAINST THE RED SOX IN 2003

You see, the Mets are losers, just like nearly everybody else in life. This is the team for the cab driver who gets held up and the guy who loses out on a promotion because he didn't maneuver himself to lunch with the boss enough. It is the team for every guy who has to get out of bed in the morning and go to work for short money on a job he does not like. Who does well enough to root for them, Laurence Rockefeller?

JIMMY BRESLIN IN *CAN'T ANYBODY HERE PLAY THIS GAME?*

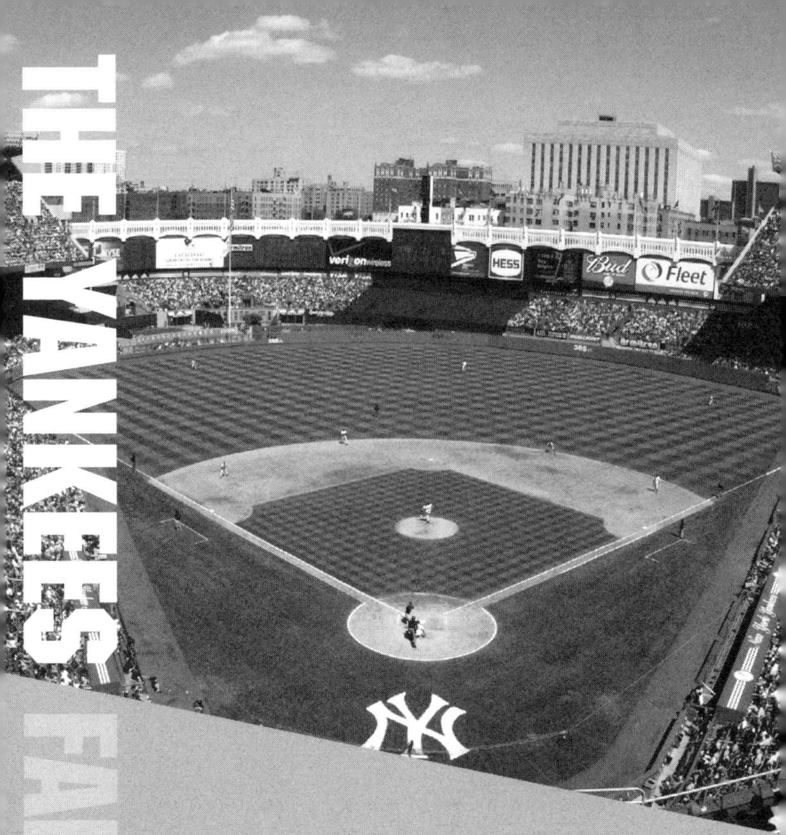

OPPONENTS AND YANKEES HATERS

Yankees Trivia

The opponent for the first game ever at Yankee Stadium (April 18, 1923) was, of course, the Boston Red Sox.

There are many Yankees opponents whom I respect and appreciate. Guys like Bill Mazeroski and George Brett, Juan Gonzalez and Curt Schilling, Randy Johnson and Manny Ramirez, Pedro Martinez and Pudge Rodriguez will live forever in my mind as Yankees killers. They made the games interesting because they've got game. On the other hand, it always feels good when we extract our revenge from these guys. Brett got pine tarred and Juan

Gone was always gone by the end of the American League Division Series, sent packing back to the Lone Star State! Pedro will forever be remembered, as much for his competitive fire as the way he coughed it up in the seventh inning of Game Seven in 2003. You're right, Pedro: we are your daddy! But at least Pedro played the game and played it well, I might add. The Yankees haters out there don't play the game. They just had the misfortune of being raised to root for some other team. And for this, they blame us and our beloved Bronx Bombers.

They hate the rings. They hate the pomp and they hate the circumstance, the circumstance being that a lot of money comes the Yankees' way because of the team's geographic location. YES Network can demand big bucks as a premier cable channel, and a seat in the upper decks now costs an arm and a leg and the other arm, too. But we pay it because we like to see good baseball. And besides, other teams could follow the Yankee model, which, according to all opponent and hater arguments should mean instant success. Last time I checked, the Phillies, Cubs, and Dodgers are in pretty big media markets. When the Angels, who can't even figure out where they're from, won it all, there went the Dodgers' excuse. Same with the Cubs after the Pale Hose brought it home. The bottom line is: don't hate the Yankees because they put money back into the franchise. And don't hate them because they've found success where your team has not. Maybe you should be angry with your owner and your management. Maybe you should write a letter or start a fan campaign. This might be a more productive use of your time, Yankees hater. More productive than bashing the Yankees.

I would rather pitch a double-header against any other club than one game against the Yanks.

MILT GASTON

Those fellows not only beat you, but they tear your hearts out.

JOE JUDGE

Ruppert bought some pennants when he was able to reach out to the Red Sox for players. But it doesn't seem to work for us when we buy old champions. So, we've got to do something else and raise our own. . . . That's the only way we can catch the Yankees.

TOM YAWKEY

He stopped everything **behind the plate and hit everything in front of it.**

MEL OTT, DESCRIBING YANKEE CATCHER YOGI BERRA

As much as we disliked the Yankees, fans and players alike, they were good for baseball. The consistently unsuccessful teams . . . paid a lot of their bills with those big crowds that poured through the gates when the Yankees came to town.

BOB FELLER

Allie Reynolds was a peach of a guy. . . . If you didn't love Yogi Berra or Phil Rizzuto, there was something wrong with you.

JOHNNY PESKY

Every time I see a Yankee hat, I see a swastika just a little off kilter.

BILL LEE

The more self-centered and egotistical a guy is, the better ballplayer he's going to be. You take a team with twenty-five assholes and I'll show you a pennant. I'll show you the New York Yankees.

BILL LEE

I could never play in New York. The first time I came into a game there, I got into the bullpen car and they told me to lock the doors.

MIKE FLANAGAN

The Yankees are together as a unit and we are not. . . . The way I see it, the Yanks had a guy, Jackson, who comes out of the hospital to play in the series against us. That's how much it meant to them. We have a guy who pulls himself out of a game after making a couple of errors.

RICK BURLESON, DESCRIBING HIS 1978 RED SOX TEAM

Note: The player who pulled himself out was Dwight Evans, although it sure sounds a lot like a reference to Manny Ramirez!

The Royals and the Yankees hated each other. To this day, whenever I see Lou Piniella or one of those Yankees, we talk about how we hated those guys. One time I didn't even have the ball and Piniella tried to spike me at third base.

GEORGE BRETT

They can't get any rougher on us unless they show up with Uzis.

DAVID JUSTICE, COMMENTING ON THE YANKEE STADIUM CROWD AS A MEMBER OF THE CLEVELAND INDIANS

The Yankees are head and shoulders above. We don't deserve the blame. They deserve the credit.

JOHN SMOLTZ, AFTER LOSING THE 1999 WORLD SERIES

I can tell when George Steinbrenner is lying. His lips are moving.

JERRY REINSDORF

I guess **I hate the Yankees now.**

CURT SCHILLING, UPON SIGNING WITH THE RED SOX IN 2003

When you play the Yankees, you have to do everything right. Pitching, defense, offense. You can't allow opportunities to pass. You can't give them more than 27 outs in a game.

CURT SCHILLING

They're great players, they did what they had to do to win a ballgame. I respect them for that, I respect the way they play. There's nothing I could say bad against those guys.

PEDRO MARTINEZ, AFTER LOSING GAME SEVEN IN THE 2003 AMERICAN LEAGUE CHAMPIONSHIP SERIES

I wish I'd never see them again. I wish they'd disappear from the league. Then we'd be winners.

PEDRO MARTINEZ

We know that to get to the World Series we have to go through the Yankees at one point or another.

THEO EPSTEIN

The evil empire **extends its tentacles even into Latin America.**

LARRY LUCCHINO, RED SOX TEAM PRESIDENT, REVEALING HIS DEEP-ROOTED YANKEES PARANOIA.

Note: The Boss's response to Lucchino was: "That's B.S. That's how a sick person thinks."

I recognize that they are what's evil in sports. Its not that there's hatred, but this is the epicenter of all things that are wrong with professional sports embodied by George Steinbrenner.

BEN AFFLECK, WHOSE CURRENT STREAK OF CINEMATIC FLOPS COULD BE DESCRIBED AS THE "CURSE OF THE BENBINO!"

Armed robbery hardly turns a head in the mostly lawless bleachers, where warlords and tribal law prevail.

BILL MAHONEY, OF CALLOFTHEGREENMONSTER.COM (A FEEBLE RIPOFF OF THE PARODIES OF THEONION.COM)

Hating the Yankees is as American as pizza pie, unwed mothers, and cheating on your income tax.

MIKE ROYKO

THE YANKEES FANATIC

ENHANCING YOUR
FANATIC EXPERIENCE

If you're going to the Stadium, gates open two hours before game time. Monument Park closes anywhere from forty-five minutes to one hour before the game.

When having fun with the family, remember that all children over thirty inches tall must have a ticket to gain entry to the Stadium.

Not that I'm suggesting you measure or anything, but . . . if you're a little large in the derriere, the seats at Yankee Stadium are twenty-two inches wide. Before complaining, though, it's worth mentioning that they were eighteen inches wide (and made of wood!) before the remodeling in 1975.

For information on Stadium tours, go to http://newyork.yankees.mlb.com/NASApp/mlb/nyy/ballpark/stadium_tours.jsp,

call the Yankee Stadium Tours Department at 718-579-4531,

or E-mail tmorante@yankees.com.

The following items are banned at Yankee Stadium: beach balls; blow horns and all other distracting noisemakers (except for Freddie Sez and his tin pan); briefcases, attaché cases, or any type of bags and/or large purses; firearms and/or knives; glass or plastic bottles, cans, coolers, and/or containers; laptops; laser pens/pointers; smoking; video cameras or handhelds.

A "Fan Marquee" message displayed during a game costs $100, and only ten messages will be displayed, so it's first come, first served. Scoreboard messages are only $10. For more information, go to http://newyork.yankees.mlb.com/NASApp/mlb/nyy/ballpark/stadium_messages.jsp, call 718-579-4464, or E-mail scoreboard@yankees.com.

If you want to sing the National Anthem before a game, send an audiotape to:

Special Events Department
Anthem Records
Yankee Stadium
Bronx, NY 10451

The mailing address for Yankee Stadium is:
161st Street and River Avenue
Bronx, NY 10451

For a free fan gift package (information, schedule, pictures, stickers), send a postcard to:

Yankees Fan Mail Department
Yankee Stadium
Bronx, NY 10451

To write to a specific player:

Player's Name
Yankee Stadium
Bronx, NY 10451

To join the fan club go to http://secure.mlb.com/NASApp/mlb/nyy/fan_forum/fanclub.jsp. Membership is $26 a year.

To order any of the Yankees publications: http://secure.mlb.com/NASApp/mlb/nyy/fan_forum/publications.jsp or call 1-800-GO-YANKS.

The Stadium is available for off-season events. You can even get married at home plate!

Call Gina Chindemi at 718-579-4416 or E-mail events@yankees.com.

File it under "Adult Fun": it's Fantasy Camp at Legends Field! To get information and/or sign up, call 1-800-368-CAMP.

To inquire about spring training tickets, call 813-879-2244. The games are played in Tampa, Florida, at Legends Field.

YANKEES QUIZ

OK, Yankees Fanatics, it's time to test your Bronx Bomber IQ. If you get off to a rough start, fear not. I made sure there were some multiple-choice questions to go along with the tough ones. Good luck!

THE NICKNAMES

These fifteen players certainly aren't the only Yankees to have nicknames. Jeet and Donnie Baseball might not be included, but you will find Yankees from every era. Match the player and the name, then find out just how much you know about your Yankees and their nicknames. Ten correct and the Yankees will retire your number. Fifteen correct and you're a first-ballot Hall of Famer.

Lou Gehrig
Ron Guidry
Jim Hunter
Phil Rizzuto
David Wells
Orlando Hernandez
Joe DiMaggio
Reggie Jackson
Miller Huggins
Graig Nettles
Ralph Houk
Bill Skowron
Jim Bouton
Eddie Lopat
Charles Ruffing

El Duque
The Junkman
Bulldog
Moose
Mr. October
Scooter
The Mighty Mite
The Major
Yankee Clipper
Red
Iron Horse
Puff
Catfish
Louisiana Lightnin'
Boomer

ANSWERS

Lou Gehrig (Iron Horse)
Ron Guidry (Louisiana Lightnin')
Jim Hunter (Catfish)
David Wells (Boomer)
Orlando Hernandez (El Duque)
Joe DiMaggio (Yankee Clipper)
Reggie Jackson (Mr. October)
Miller Huggins (The Mighty Mite)
Graig Nettles (Puff)
Ralph Houk (The Major)
Bill Skowron (Moose)
Jim Bouton (Bulldog)
Eddie Lopat (The Junkman)
Charles Ruffing (Red)
Phil Rizzuto (Scooter).

THE YANKEE CAPTAINS

Fill in the last name of each of the eleven Yankee captains. They are listed in chronological order.

Hal ______________________

Roger ______________________

Babe ______________________

Everett ______________________

Lou ______________________

Thurman ______________________

Graig ______________________

Willie ______________________

Ron ______________________

Don ______________________

Derek ______________________

ANSWERS

Hal Chase (1912)
Roger Peckinpaugh (1914–1921)
Babe Ruth (5/20/1922–5/25/1922)
Everett Scott (1922–1925)
Lou Gehrig (1935–1941)
Thurman Munson (1976–1979)
Graig Nettles (1982–1984)
Willie Randolph (1986–1989)
Ron Guidry (1986–1989)
Don Mattingly (1991–1995)
Derek Jeter (2003–present)

THE BRONX BOMBERS

Can you name the eight Yankees who have been the American League home run champ?

Answers: The following are the Yankees' American League home run champions as of 2006: Babe Ruth (nine times); Lou Gehrig (three times); Joe DiMaggio (twice); Mickey Mantle (four times); Roger Maris (once); Graig Nettles (once); Reggie Jackson (once); Alex Rodriguez (once).

PICK A YEAR, ANY YEAR!

The New York Highlanders first used the interlocking *NY* emblem in what year?

a) 1903

b) 1909

c) 1912

d) 1920

Answer: b. The interlocking NY first appeared in 1909.

In what year was the original interlocking NY designed?

a) 1877

b) 1897

c) 1907

d) 1909

Answer: a. In 1877 Louis B. Tiffany designed a medal for the first New York City police officer who was shot in the line of duty. The team's owner, Bill Devery, was a former police chief so that might be why he liked the design.

In what year did George Steinbrenner buy the Yankees from CBS?

a) 1973

b) 1972

c) 1971

d) 1970

Answer: a. The Boss bought the Yankees from CBS in 1973.

In what year did the Yankees defeat the Mets in the "Subway Series?"

a) 1998

b) 1999

c) 2000

d) 2001

Answer: c. The Yankees beat the Mets in the Subway Series in 2000, breaking hearts all over Queens. Too bad!

In which two consecutive years did the Yankees play the Red Sox in a deciding Game Seven of the American League Championship Series?

---

a) 2002 and 2003

b) 2001 and 2002

c) 2004 and 2005

d) 2003 and 2004

Answer: d. In 2003 Aaron Boone put the BoSox to bed, but in 2004 pigs flew over The Bronx and the devil got to throw his first snowball.

In what year was Jason Giambi named the American League Comeback Player of the Year?

a) 2004

b) 2005

c) 1999

d) 2001

Answer: b. In 2005 Jason Giambi came back strong, slugging thirty-two home runs and knocking in eighty-seven RBIs.

In what year did Don Mattingly set records for consecutive games with a home run (eight) and most grand slams in a season (six)?

---

a) 1987

b) 1988

c) 1989

d) 1990

Answer: a. In 1987 Donnie Baseball set those two records. He also won a Gold Glove.

In what year did David Wells throw a perfect game against the Minnesota Twins?

a) 1998

b) 1999

c) 1997

d) 2000

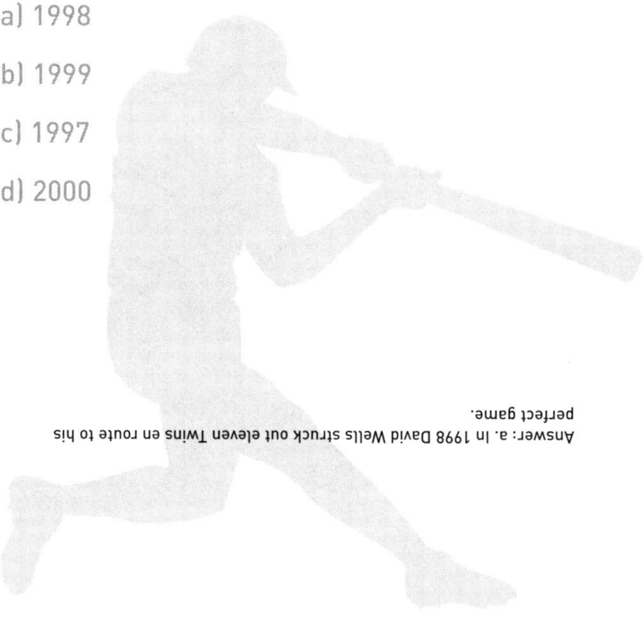

Answer: a. In 1998 David Wells struck out eleven Twins en route to his perfect game.

In what year did David Cone throw a perfect game against the Montreal Expos?

a) 1997

b) 1998

c) 1999

d) 1996

Answer: c. In 1999 David Cone faced the minimum number of Expos (including three at bats for Vladimir Guerrero) for his perfecto.

In what year did one-handed pitcher Jim Abbott throw a no-hitter against the Cleveland Indians?

a) 1989

b) 1991

c) 1993

d) 1995

Answer: c. Jim Abbott became front-page news when he threw his no-hitter against the Tribe in 1993.

In what year did the Yankees win their first World Series?

a) 1919

b) 1923

c) 1925

d) 1927

Answer: b. The Yankees won their first championship in 1923, defeating the New York Giants four games to two.

In what year were lights added to Yankee Stadium?

---

a) 1946

b) 1947

c) 1948

d) 1949

Answer: a. Yankee Stadium brought night baseball to the Bronx in 1946.

In what year did Lou Gehrig win the Triple Crown?

a) 1930

b) 1932

c) 1934

d) 1936

Answer: c. The Iron Horse won the Triple Crown in 1934 with forty-nine homers, 165 RBIs, and a .363 batting average.

In what year was Mariano Rivera the World Series MVP?

a) 1996

b) 1997

c) 1998

d) 1999

Answer: d. In 1999 the Yankees swept the Braves and Mo earned the MVP award.

In what year was Monument Park first opened?

a) 1913

b) 1932

c) 1954

d) 1978

Answer: b. Monument Park opened in 1932. Manager Miller Huggins was honored with the first plaque.

In what year did Ron Blomberg become the first-ever designated hitter?

a) 1973

b) 1974

c) 1975

d) 1976

Answer: a. In 1973 Ron Blomberg became baseball's first designated hitter.
He walked in that first at bat.

In what year did the Yankees become the first professional sports team to travel by airplane?

a) 1936

b) 1941

c) 1946

d) 1951

Answer: c. In 1946, the Yankees flew the friendly skies for the first time—the same year that they added lights to The House That Ruth Built.

In what year did Bernie Williams win the American League batting title with a .339 average?

a) 2000

b) 1998

c) 1999

d) 2001

Answer: b. Bernie won the title in 1998. Bern baby bern!

CALLING ALL ALL-STARS

In which three years did Yankee Stadium host the all-star game?

Answer: Yankee Stadium played host to the all-star game in 1939, 1960, and 1977.

YANKEE GREATNESS

By clinching the American League East in 2006, how many division titles in a row had the Yankees won?

Answer: Nine, count 'em, nine. Kind of makes it hard for Mets and Red Sox fans to talk about success and excellence, doesn't it?

As of 2006, how many championships have the Yankees won?

Answer: They have won twenty-six championships while appearing in the World Series thirty-nine times. They brought the trophy home to the Bronx in 1923, 1927, 1928, 1932, 1936, 1937, 1938, 1939, 1941, 1943, 1947, 1949, 1950, 1951, 1952, 1953, 1956, 1958, 1961, 1962, 1977, 1978, 1996, 1998, 1999, and 2000.

As of 2005, how many former Yankee players and managers have been elected to baseball's Hall of Fame?

Answer: Forty-two and that doesn't include the Hall of Famers who only wore the pinstripes for one season.

How long was Lou Gehrig's consecutive game streak?

Answer: 2,130 games.

In 1927, Babe Ruth hit his record-setting sixty home runs but did not lead the team in RBIs. Who did?

Answer: Lou Gehrig led the team with 175 RBIs. Ruth had 164.

In Casey Stengel's first five years of managing the Yankees, how many world championships did they win?

Answer: Five, count 'em, five. Yep, between 1949 and 1953 the Yankees won all five championships.

Mickey Mantle hit 536 career home runs, the most ever by a switch hitter. Did he hit more from the left side or the right side?

Answer: Mantle hit 373 left-handed home runs and 163 right-handed.

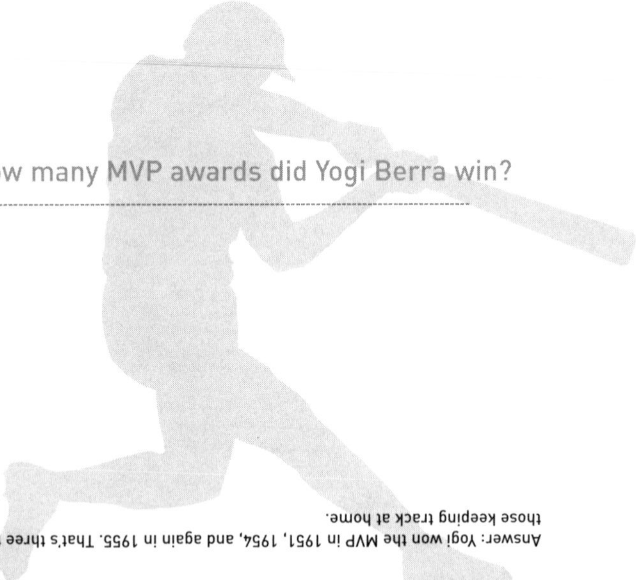

How many MVP awards did Yogi Berra win?

Answer: Yogi won the MVP in 1951, 1954, and again in 1955. That's three for those keeping track at home.

On what date did Don Larsen pitch his perfect game?

Answer: On October 8, 1956. I won't ever get tired of watching Yogi leap into Larson's arms instead of vice versa.

On what date did Reggie Jackson hit his three Game Six World Series home runs?

Answer: On October 18, 1977. He hit them off Burt Hooton, Elias Sosa, and Charlie Hough.

Who managed the Yankees to four consecutive World Series championships between 1936 and 1939?

Answer: Joe McCarthy

When Ron Guidry won the Cy Young Award in 1978, how many games did he win?

Answer: He was 25-3 with a 1.74 ERA. He had 248 strikeouts and I got to see eighteen of them against the Angels!

How many Gold Glove awards did Don Mattingly win between 1982 and 1995?

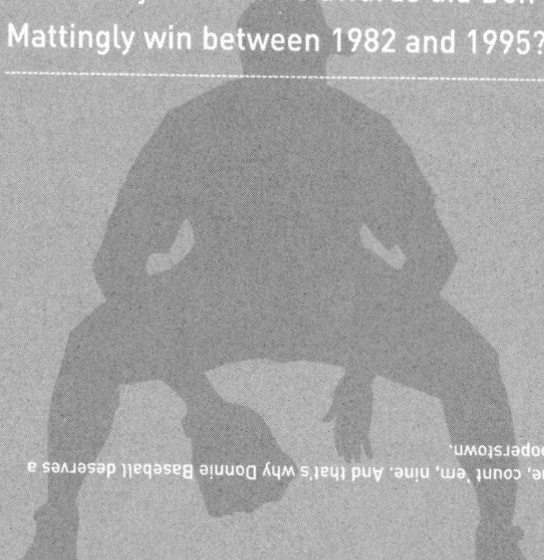

Answer: Nine, count 'em, nine. And that's why Donnie Baseball deserves a plaque in Cooperstown.

During which four-year span did Bernie Williams win four consecutive Gold Glove awards?

Answer: After displacing Roberto Kelly, Bernie took over in center field and went on to win Gold Gloves every year between 1997 and 2000.

Jorge Posada entered the Yankee minor league system playing what position?

Answer: In his first season in Oneonta, New York, he played sixty-four games at second base and eleven games as catcher.

Can you name all of the plaques in Monument Park?

Answer: Each of the following men has a plaque in Monument Park: owner Jacob Ruppert; general manager Ed Barrow; managers Miller Huggins and Joe McCarthy; broadcaster Mel Allen; public address announcer Bob Sheppard; the victims and rescue workers of the 9/11 attacks; Pope Paul VI and Pope John Paul II (to commemorate the Masses they said in Yankee Stadium); position players Lou Gehrig, Babe Ruth, Joe DiMaggio, Mickey Mantle, Thurman Munson, Elston Howard, Roger Maris, Phil Rizzuto, Billy Martin, Bill Dickey, Yogi Berra, Don Mattingly, and Reggie Jackson; and pitchers Red Ruffing, Lefty Gomez, Allie Reynolds, Whitey Ford, and Ron Guidry.

WHAT'S IN A NAME?

Name the Yankee pitcher who lost 4–0 to the White Sox (1990) despite throwing a no-hitter.

Answer: Andy Hawkins suffered the effects of two errors and lost the game. Ouch.

Name the two general managers whose efforts led to the dynasty teams of the 1990s?

Answer: Gene Michael (1990–1995) and Bob Watson (1995–1998). Watson was the first African-American GM to ever win a World Series title.

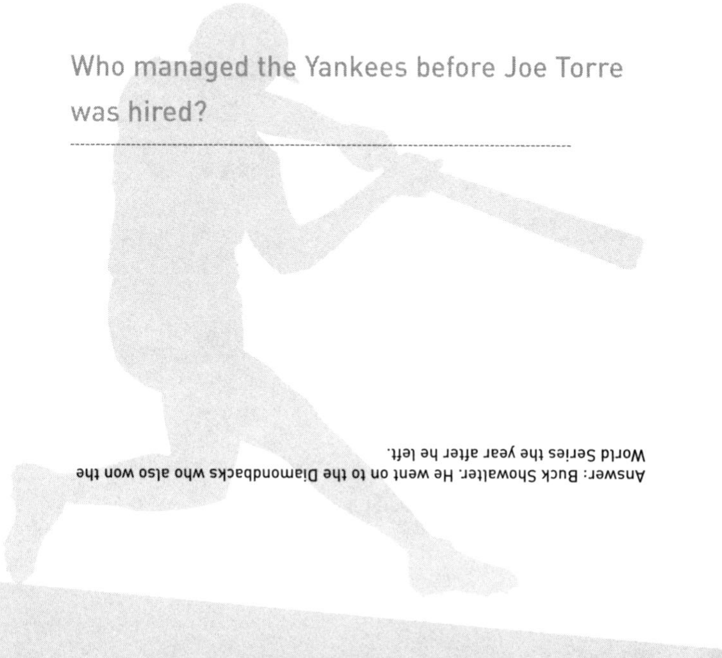

Who managed the Yankees before Joe Torre was hired?

Answer: Buck Showalter. He went on to the Diamondbacks who also won the World Series the year after he left.

Name the Yankee Stadium organist who retired after the 2003 season.

Answer: Eddie Layton tickled the ivories for the Yankees for almost forty years before retiring in 2003.

BY THE NUMBERS

In which year did the Yankees become the first team to make numbers a permanent part of the uniform?

Answer: In 1929 the Yankees gave individual players a number and that number indicated where the player fell in the batting order. For example, Babe Ruth was the number 3 hitter.

How tall is the Louisville Slugger bat outside The Stadium and what is its real purpose?

Answer: 120 feet tall and it's a boiler stack.

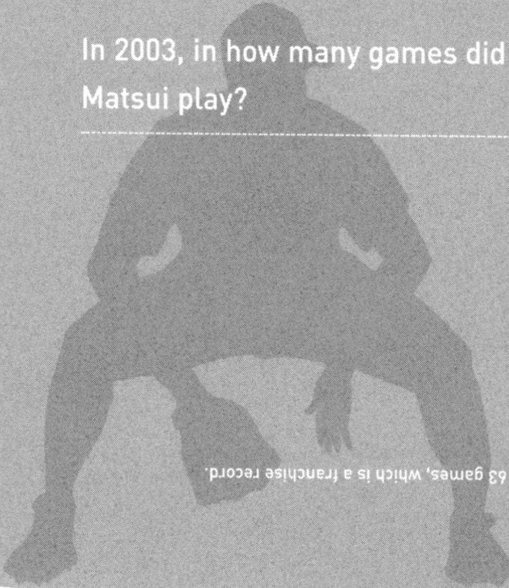

In 2003, in how many games did Hideki Matsui play?

Answer: He played in 163 games, which is a franchise record.

Who is the only active player in baseball allowed to wear the number 42?

Answer: Mariano Rivera. The number 42 is retired in honor of Jackie Robinson, but since Rivera was wearing 42 before Major League Baseball's decision, he can use it until he retires.

OUR FAVORITE RETIREES

Match the player with the retired number.

1	Lou Gehrig
3	Casey Stengel
4	Mickey Mantle
5	Thurman Munson
7	Reggie Jackson
8	Whitey Ford
8	Roger Maris
9	Bill Dickey
10	Yogi Berra
15	Elston Howard
16	Jackie Robinson
23	Ron Guidry
32	Billy Martin
37	Don Mattingly
42	Babe Ruth
44	Phil Rizzuto
49	Joe DiMaggio

ANSWERS:

1 Billy Martin (2B, manager)
3 Babe Ruth (OF)
4 Lou Gehrig (1B)
5 Joe DiMaggio (OF)
7 Mickey Mantle (OF)
8 Yogi Berra (C)
8 Bill Dickey (C)
9 Roger Maris (OF)
10 Phil Rizzuto (SS)
15 Thurman Munson (C)
16 Whitey Ford (P)
23 Don Mattingly (1B)
32 Elston Howard (C)
37 Casey Stengel (M)
42 Jackie Robinson (2B)
44 Reggie Jackson (OF)
49 Ron Guidry (P)

THE CLOSER: LOSERS DON'T CAUSE TRAFFIC JAMS

There's a reason every bridge and tunnel leading into New York experiences backups before a game and in the outbound lanes after a game. The Yankees are winners and people love to see a winner.

They love coming out to watch Jeter and his intangibles, on full display, on the grandest stage in all of baseball. They love coming out to experience traditions like the ground crew's "YMCA" during the fifth inning, and Sinatra's "New York, New York," after a win. (Booooooooo, Liza Minelli. Her version can be heard after Yankee losses.) They love coming out to share the Yankee Stadium experience with their kids and they love coming out for a fun night with friends or business associates. But most of all, they love coming because they're fans. I know that that's why I go, why I've always gone, why I will continue to go. It's why I'll bring my kids as soon as they're old enough to appreciate sac flies and the changeup. Not yet, though. I can deal with all the traffic, but not three innings of trying to track down a foam finger. When the time finally comes, I'll have a sit-down with the loin fruit and explain how much traffic fifty thousand plus people can cause. And why it'll be the beginning of a beeeeeautiful relationship between baseball and them. Who knows what jersey number they'll someday pick. . . .

When you root for a loser, traffic's rarely a problem. There are a couple of diehards with season tickets and a couple of walk ups but never a crowd. At least not until the Bronx Bombers show up in their road grays. The Yankees aren't just a joy to behold for their fans. Even their opponents, including those who claim to hate the Yankees, love them. Even the fans of the opposing team dig them. It's true. Tickets might be a little harder to come by when the Yankees come to town, and the traffic might be a little worse than usual, but everybody knows it's well worth it. To see the Evil Empire in action? To see a winner, live and in the flesh? Oh yes, the masses will show. Out of curiosity, for love or for hate, they'll come out to the ballpark. Yep, even if it's for hate they'll shell out the extra money (many teams charge more for Yankees games). These are the same people who bought the *Why I Hate the Yankees* book. Who ever heard of spending money on something you hate? Crazy.

There's another reason the fans come out to see the Bronx Bombers. They serve as a basis of comparison. The Yankees have the competitive bull's-eye on their backs and, thus, are baseball's measuring stick. Yankees haters are always tuned in to what the Yankees are doing, and as they're sitting in the stands, watching their beloved B Leaguers take on the Evil Empire, they can determine how their team stacks up. And my oh my if something good happens . . . if their team can beat the Yankees, they think that their team is good. If their big bopper takes a pinstriped pitcher deep, they think that they've taught our boys some sort of "live by the sword, die by the sword" lesson. If their rookie pitcher holds his own against the

Bronx Bombers, they think that the future looks bright. If their team goes farther than the Yankees in the postseason, they think that it's been a great season. No matter what happens in the next round.

But, more often than not, their team loses and then those hatin' fans have to leave for home. It takes a while to get there, though, because the influx of people causes so much traffic. As they sit in that traffic, bumper to bumper, and have to read some sort of Yankees championship bumper sticker on the car in front, they can talk about how their closer gave it up in the ninth or how their starter was so bad that the Yankees reserves were playing by the sixth inning. There will be little shock in their voices as everybody, from opposing players to management to fans, expects to lose to the Yankees. No one's surprised when the Yankees take two out of three, three out of five, or in October, four out of seven. The haters can write their loss off as a valiant effort; a moral victory; a cause that was doomed from the start against that team with the highest payroll. What a bunch of baloney.

When the Yankees lose, they don't make excuses. Beat Kevin Brown in the 1998 World Series and we have to hear how he has the flu. Watch Mariano give the home run up to Sandy Alomar or the bloop to Luis Gonzalez and all he does is walk off the mound, calmly describe the pitch he wanted to throw, what went wrong, and how he'll have forgotten about it by tomorrow. And he means it. O'Neill might kick over the water cooler, the Big Unit might want to rip a reporter's head off, but at least they don't give any sort of convoluted reason for their failure. And for more than ten years now, this has been an approach—a philosophy, if you will—that transcends the team from manager to rookies. After a loss, Torre backs up his players, gives props to the other manager, admits how much losing bothers him, and then turns the page. Fortunately, the Yankees team and the Yankees fans are used to seeing a victory on that next page. The Jeters and Marianos always find a way to win. They always manage to lead us out of the desert. Or at least make the traffic less painful after another exciting win!

Simply put, the Yankees are the team all others are measured by. They are, hands down, the most respected team in baseball. And the Yankees fans, from the upper decks to the Bleacher Creatures, the luxury boxes to the box seats, from the Deegan to the Bruckner, know that they have the best team in baseball. In turn, I can't help but think that the team knows that they have the best fans in all of baseball. It's a symbiotic relationship with the fans getting amped up about player performance and the players getting amped up when the crowd gets loud: "Let's go Yankees!" Clap! Clap! Clapclapclap!!! Long live the Yankees and long live the Yankees Fanatics.

The Yankee pinstripes, they stay with you wherever you go.

BILLY MARTIN

INDEX